The Scottish National Party

The Scottish National Party

Transition to Power

James Mitchell, Lynn Bennie, and Rob Johns

OXFORD
UNIVERSITY PRESS

OXFORD

UNIVERSITY PRESS

Great Clarendon Street, Oxford OX2 6DP

Oxford University Press is a department of the University of Oxford.
It furthers the University's objective of excellence in research, scholarship,
and education by publishing worldwide in

Oxford New York

Auckland Cape Town Dar es Salaam Hong Kong Karachi
Kuala Lumpur Madrid Melbourne Mexico City Nairobi
New Delhi Shanghai Taipei Toronto

With offices in

Argentina Austria Brazil Chile Czech Republic France Greece
Guatemala Hungary Italy Japan Poland Portugal Singapore
South Korea Switzerland Thailand Turkey Ukraine Vietnam

Oxford is a registered trade mark of Oxford University Press
in the UK and in certain other countries

Published in the United States
by Oxford University Press Inc., New York

British Library Cataloguing in Publication Data
Data available

Library of Congress Cataloging in Publication Data
Data available

Typeset by SPI Publisher Services, Pondicherry, India
Printed in Great Britain
on acid-free paper by
MPG Books Group, Bodmin and King's Lynn

ISBN 978–0–19–958000–2

3 5 7 9 10 8 6 4

Acknowledgements

We would like to acknowledge the support of the Economic and Social Research Council (ESRC) for this project (RES-062-23-0722). In addition, we are grateful to the Scottish National Party (SNP) for allowing us access to its membership list. We are especially grateful to Peter Murrell, SNP chief executive and Ian McCann of SNP headquarters for responding to numerous queries and facilitating the completion of this research. We are also grateful to the following members and former member of the SNP who agreed to be interviewed:

Brian Adam, Alasdair Allan, David Berry, Ian Blackford, Keith Brown, Aileen Campbell, Angela Constance, Bruce Crawford, Ewan Crawford, Roseanna Cunningham, Jennifer Dempsie, Noel Dollan, Nigel Don, Bob Doris, James Dornan, Fergus Ewing, Linda Fabiani, John Fellowes, Gareth Finn, Gerry Fisher, Joe Fitzpatrick, Stephen Gethins, Kenneth Gibson, Rob Gibson, Christine Grahame, James Halliday, Duncan Hamilton, Christopher Harvie, William Henderson, Jamie Hepburn, Julie Hepburn, Stewart Hosie, Alison Hunter, Fiona Hyslop, Adam Ingram, Bill Kidd, Liz Lloyd, Richard Lochhead, Jim Lynch, Kenny MacAskill, Margo MacDonald, John MacInnes, Derek Mackay, Angus MacNeil, Tricia Marwick, John Mason, Jim Mather, Michael Matheson, Stewart Maxwell, Ian McCann, John McFarlane, Ian McKee, Christina McKelvie, Anne McLaughlin, Stuart McMillan, Anne McNair, Alasdair Morgan, Peter Murrell, Alex Neil, Stephen Noon, Gil Paterson, Kevin Pringle, David Purves, Angus Robertson, Shona Robison, Duncan Ross, Michael Russell, Alex Salmond, Mark Shaw, Alyn Smith, Shirley-Anne Somerville, Chris Stevens, Stewart Stevenson, Kevin Stewart, Nicola Sturgeon, John Swinney, Alison Thewliss, Dave Thompson, Grant Thoms, Maureen Watt, Andrew Welsh, Sandra White, Eilidh Whiteford, Bill Wilson, Gordon Wilson, and John Wilson.

We appreciated comments on earlier drafts of the survey from Kevin Adamson, Alistair Clark, Iain Docherty, Grant Jordan, Enric Martínez-Herrera, Colin Mackay, David McCrone, Brendan O'Hara, Lindsay Paterson, Wolfgang Rüdig, Roger Scully, Mark Shephard, Anders Widfeldt, and Alex Wright. Address Data Solutions (ADS) Ltd provided the mailing and data entry services for the project. The main challenge we faced on receipt of the data was interpreting our open-ended question asking why members had joined the party. We are grateful to Arno van der Zwet for assisting in this major enterprise. It was a massive task but well worth the effort allowing us to see what members themselves had to say. We are grateful to Arno and Nicola McEwen for comments on an earlier draft of this book.

We produced a number of conference and seminar papers and work on these and, most importantly, feedback at these conferences has been very helpful. We are grateful for the opportunity to present our findings at the Political Studies Association's annual conferences in 2009 and 2010; the American Political Science Association annual conferences in 2008 and 2009; Elections, Public Opinion, and Parties annual conferences in 2008 and 2009. Findings were also presented at seminars at Queens University, Belfast and University of Cardiff, both in 2009 with helpful feeedback in each case.

JM, LB, RJ

Contents

List of Tables

List of Tables

List of Figures

1

Introduction

Introduction

This book has a number of objectives. Its primary objective is to contribute to our understanding of the Scottish National Party (SNP). The SNP was elected to govern Scotland in May 2007, almost eighty years after it was founded. For most of its history, the party was on the fringe of Scottish politics and even when it became a significant force in Scottish politics it remained on the fringe of British politics. The party's presence in the House of Commons at Westminster has been precarious. The establishment of a Scottish Parliament in 1999 altered the 'opportunity structure' (McAdam, 1996: 27), giving the SNP the chance both to become a secure Parliamentary party and to have the prospect of being in government. However, devolution alone does not explain the SNP's election success in 2007. The SNP had also undergone significant internal change. This book explores the kind of party the SNP had become by the time it was elected to power. The evolving organizational structure of the party is explored, including the relationship between party elites, activists, and passive members. Our central argument is that the SNP had become an electoral professional party with a membership to match by the time it won the 2007 Scottish Parliament elections. Its organization had changed from being the amateur activist party that it had been up to and for a few years after devolution. By 2007, its membership was pragmatic, though independence motivated its members and activists. This pragmatism was evident across a range of policy issues as well as in pursuing its goal of independence. The book is based on a study that was conducted at a particular moment in the party's history and it is likely that in different circumstances, such as following a major electoral defeat, its members might adopt different positions.

At such an important time for the SNP, remarkably little is known about the party and especially its wider membership. Until now,

1

research on the SNP has focused on its historical development, electoral support, and political strategy (Hanham, 1969; Brand, 1978; Levy, 1990; Finlay, 1994; Mitchell, 1996; Bennie et al., 1997; Brown et al., 1999; Paterson et al., 2001; Lynch, 2002; McEwen, 2002; Clark, 2006; Paterson, 2006; Johns et al., 2010). Very little is known about the characteristics or motivations of the SNP's members and little has been written about members' roles within the party's organization. In particular, little is known about the transition from being a small oppositional force, heavily dependent on voluntary activity into a party of government. The book will make this information available while complementing studies of other parties in the United Kingdom (Rüdig et al., 1991; Seyd and Whiteley, 1992, 1995, 2002; Whiteley et al., 1994; Bennie et al., 1996; Rüdig et al., 1996; Whiteley and Seyd, 1998; Tonge and Evans, 2001, 2002; Bennie, 2004; Murray and Tonge, 2005; Tonge, 2005, 2006; Whiteley et al., 2006).

Members are vital to the SNP, as for any party. They provide financial backing, participate in policy development, help attract electoral support, and supply senior and elected officials. However, it could be argued that members are especially important to the SNP. As indicated in Chapter 2, this is a party which has traditionally been seen as having social movement roots, relying heavily on its members for financial support, campaign activities, and contributions to internal decision-making (Mansbach, 1972; Brand, 1978, 1992; Crawford, 1982; Levy, 1990; Mitchell, 1996). Furthermore, the SNP has reported year-on-year increases in members since 2003, at a time of an apparent 'spiral of decline' in membership numbers in other parties, both in Britain and elsewhere, noted in academic research. Dalton and Wattenberg (2000: 3) point to 'mounting evidence' of a declining role for political parties in 'shaping the politics of advanced industrial democracies' and the public becoming 'increasingly sceptical about partisan politics'. A central component of such claims is a widespread decline in both membership numbers and activity rates of those who join parties (Mair and Van Beizen, 2001; Webb et al., 2002; Seyd and Whiteley, 2004; Morales, 2009; Whiteley, 2009; Scarrow and Gezgor, 2010). Reports of the decline of political parties have also been common in the media. In late 2010, the *Economist* referred to the 'withering' of party membership though the paper questioned whether this was necessarily bad news (*Economist*, 23 October 2010). Some portray these trends as convenient for party leaders, allowing them strategic freedom, while a body of literature has emerged to defend the importance of members, the view being that members are vital to a party. Members provide financial backing, participate in policy development, help attract electoral support, and supply senior and elected officials (Scarrow, 1996, 2000; Seyd and Whiteley, 2004).

Traditionally, the SNP was portrayed as an activist-based party with social movement characteristics (Mansbach, 1972; Brand, 1978; Mitchell, 1996), but in recent times the party has undergone the process of professionalization observed in other parties (Lynch, 2002). Devolution has presented the SNP with a number of opportunities, and in recent years the party has experienced organizational changes, including the implementation of a national membership register. Emerging from the 2007 Scottish Parliament elections as the largest and governing party, the SNP could also boast success in attracting members.

The book describes the demographic and socio-economic background of SNP members. We know much about who votes for the SNP but little about who joins and is active in the party. We should not expect that a party's voters will resemble its members socio-demographically or even ideologically. Nonetheless, we might expect some similarities. A considerable body of literature has explored motivations underpinning membership of parties across liberal democracies. This is used to explore motivations for joining the SNP.

The literature on nationalism is immense but much of it is speculative and lacks grounding in empirical evidence. Using a survey of the SNP's membership (see Appendix 1) and interviews with the party's elites, we are able to offer information on the political attitudes and identities of SNP members themselves. The book, therefore, contributes not only to an understanding of the SNP but also to wider debates on the structure and organization of political parties, participation in political parties, and the ideology of nationalism. The interviews were all conducted on the understanding that no interviewee would be identified. In order to protect anonymity and because it would serve little useful purpose, we have not provided dates of interviews when quotations are used (not least because at least some fellow interviewees might be able to identify other individuals quoted).

Structure of the book

Chapters 2 and 3 provide background information on the SNP and address some of the traditional theories of party organization: to what extent does the SNP conform to the amateur-activist model as it has been commonly characterized in the past or has it become a more professional party? Where does power lie in the SNP, and to what extent has the SNP become a centralized party? Recent studies of parties and their organizations point to a centralized, 'top-down' model at work in the modern party (Panebianco, 1988; Mair, 1994; Katz and Mair, 1995; Webb et al., 2002). However, the applicability of such accounts to the SNP remains untested. In Chapter 3, we also explore members' roles and influence. To what extent do ordinary members of the SNP contribute to the development of party policy, the selection of candidates, the election of party leaders, or to party campaigns? An important corollary is the extent to which members are satisfied with the distribution of power in the SNP. These opinions may be related to motivations behind activism. If members feel they can make a difference to party decision-making by being active, they are generally more likely to *be* active (Seyd and Whiteley, 2004: 360). But does being active mean that members are able to influence policymaking?

A different aspect of the elite–membership relationship concerns recruitment strategy. Studies of other parties point to a decline in member numbers and a decline in party activism. If true, these developments may have significant implications for parties and politics more generally. The SNP, however, has recently experienced a significant increase in members. This is explored in Chapter 3. It may simply be due to more efficient membership records. Alternatively, the party may be good at actively recruiting members or now has the capacity to retain members who previously drifted away.

Combining survey and interview data allows us to chart the relative positions of the party's members and elites along various attitudinal dimensions, including left–right, liberal–authoritarian, and Scotland's position in the United Kingdom. Previous studies of parties have found that such positions vary non-monotonically with level of activism: both leaders and passive members are typically less extreme or radical than the very active 'middle level' activist population. This phenomenon was termed the Law of Curvilinear Disparity by J.D. May (1973). We explore the applicability of this 'law' to the SNP. These comparisons concern not only the extremity of opinion but also its ideological coherence and consistency with official party policy. This allows for a test of whether those holding different positions within the party are in agreement on broad aims, notwithstanding differences in the radicalism with which these aims are to be pursued.

Ascertaining the demographic and socio-economic background of SNP members (in Chapter 4) allows us to build up a profile of the membership, which enables comparison with studies (both past and future) of other British parties. It also allows us to compare SNP members with SNP voters. According to voter studies, the SNP became a class party prior to devolution, in contrast to its support in the 1970s, though its appeal has since changed so that it attracted support across social classes in 2007 (Miller, 1981; Bennie et al., 1997; Johns et al., 2010). Whether different cohorts of members reflect the changing nature of SNP electoral support will be explored. As well as identifying *who* joins the SNP, the study is guided by theories relating to *why* members join a party. Chapter 5 investigates the motivations underlying respondents' decision to join. These investigations are based on established theories of political participation (see Bennie, 2004). Chapter 6 examines the nature of activism in the party. Central objectives here are to assess the *extent* of participation in the party, to map patterns and dimensions of activism, and to explore the attitudes of those who become active.

The vast theoretical literature on nationalism considers *inter alia* nationalism as doctrine, as social movement, as social–psychological identity, and in terms of its relationship to multiculturalism and liberalism. In Chapter 7, we consider these aspects of nationalism and their relevance to the SNP. Nationalism was defined by Ernest Gellner as a doctrine which holds that the 'political and national unit should be congruent' (1983: 1). What is understood by the congruence of the political and national units at the beginning of the twenty-first century amongst nationalists is not clear and worth exploring. In the late 1980s, the SNP redefined its primary constitutional objective to be 'independence in Europe', accepting European Union membership. This might seem odd from a nationalist perspective (Connor, 2001). What SNP members understand by the doctrine of nationalism today will be explored.

In addition, nationalism has been viewed as a social movement which attracts certain types of people. It might be expected that those with particular characteristics, notably native-born Scots, will be most attracted to membership of a national party but there is evidence that the SNP has managed to attract a sizeable number of Scots who are recent immigrants into Scotland, either from England or further afield (Lynch, 2002: 211–14). Early studies of Scottish nationalism suggested it attracted those who were socially dislocated (Brand, 1978). However, as already mentioned, later work showed that, at least in terms of its vote, the SNP had become a class party (Bennie et al., 1997). The SNP policy on citizenship and its general policy stances suggest that it conforms with civil or liberal nationalism, as distinct from ethnic nationalism. The underlying ethos of the party will be explored in the context of debates on nationalism and liberalism (see Beiner, 1999). We explore where the SNP membership and elites are located with respect to this ethnic–civic distinction, testing whether it is a useful distinction at all in this context. All too often, theoretical debates have taken place in an empirical vacuum with assertion and counter-assertion taking the place of empirical evidence. This study contributes to theoretical debates by providing some hard empirical data that suggests the need for theoretical refinement.

There is a literature on sub-state nationalist and regionalist parties (De Winter, 1994; De Winter and Tursan, 1998; De Winter et al., 2006; Elias and Tronconi, 2009; Hepburn, 2009; Massetti, 2009). These parties are defined in terms of their characteristics: self-contained electoral organizations fielding candidates only in those territories whose interests and identities they seek to defend (Massetti, 2009: 503) or having the core mission of pursuing 'some kind of self-government' (De Winter, 1998: 2004). The precise meaning of these objectives, as far as party members are concerned as opposed to official policy statements, has rarely been explored. Our data allows us to do this for the SNP. Political parties seeking public office, especially hoping to form a government, are required to have policies on a range of matters beyond simply representing the interests of a particular territory. Indeed, it might be contended that almost all major parties operating in liberal democracies conform with the above defining characteristics only in that the territory they represent is state- rather than sub-state-wide. This becomes more evident as a sub-state regionalist or nationalist party comes closer to governmental power and this study explores the SNP just after it had achieved governmental office.

While the party family literature may have some value in allowing comparative analysis, the comparisons we draw are with other parties operating in the same polity. In part, this reflects the lack of comparative data on other sub-state regionalist and nationalist parties but it is also because we incline to the view expressed by Mair and Muddie (1998: 222) that the diversity of ideological identities of such parties raises doubts as to the conceptual value of a regionalist party family. In exploring SNP views and attitudes across a range of policies and issues in Chapter 8, we consider where the SNP sits on the traditional left–right and authoritarian–libertarian spectrums. Understanding the SNP requires us to understand it in its own setting, how it differs, and is similar to its competitors. For SNP members, this is likely to be of paramount importance: the 'Other' against whom they define themselves denotes other political parties operating in Scotland and Britain. How these attitudes relate to the national identities of SNP members and to views on Scotland's constitutional status are explored. We conclude the book by drawing this evidence together to provide an overview of the party, returning to themes and issues outlined in this chapter.

Data and methods

This study of the SNP was funded by the Economic and Social Research Council (RES-062-23-0722). We adopted a mixed method approach, collecting both quantitative and qualitative data. The principal quantitative data collection was the first ever extensive academic survey of the SNP, timed to take advantage of the party's new centralized membership system. Responsibility for collecting subscriptions was removed from branches in January 2004 and given to the party's headquarters in Edinburgh. The target sample was the entire party membership which, at the end of 2007, stood at 13,203 members and continued to rise. The survey was conducted between November 2007 and March 2008 (more details on the data collection can be found in Appendix 2). The eventually achieved N was 7,112, a response rate of 53.9 per cent, which is similar to those obtained in several of the other party membership studies in the United Kingdom.

The design of the questionnaire ensured comparability with major social surveys, and surveys of other parties. The questionnaire included measures of demographic and socio-economic characteristics as well as existing questions on political background, activism, political attitudes, party organization, and strategy. However, the questionnaire also contained many new measures and questions unique to the SNP, notably on national identity, in order to understand the distinctive nature of the party's membership. Some of the questions on identity and constitutional preferences were drawn from existing surveys of the Scottish electorate, notably the Scottish Election Studies (Bennie et al., 1997; Brown et al., 1999; Johns et al., 2010) and the Scottish Social Attitudes surveys (Curtice et al., 2009). Where appropriate, we use these surveys to compare SNP members with those who voted for the party in 2007 and with the Scottish electorate as a whole.

The large sample size was helpful in allowing us to develop adequate subsamples. For example, an analysis of activism involves separating the sample into local office-holders, other types of activists, and passive members. The large sample also allowed us to analyse regional variations in responses. Previous party studies have been limited by their inability to explore these variations, and it is particularly important to explore local responses in the SNP due to its association with decentralized party structures and geographical diversity (Lynch, 2002). One consequence of the very large sample is that even minor differences and weak relationships achieve statistical significance. In any case, given that the respondents represent a non-random sample of more than half of the SNP membership, the conventional logic of statistical inference is not really applicable. For the most part, then, we do not report significance tests. The exceptions are large regression models, in which cell sizes are much smaller and so p-values provide a useful yardstick for judging whether predictor variables have an impact net of the other independent variables.

The central plank of qualitative data collection was a series of interviews with SNP elites, conducted between December 2007 and September 2009. Interviews, with eighty-seven members and one past member, took place ranging from 40 minutes to 4 hours in length. Some party officials were interviewed on a number of occasions. The interviews involved the following groups: SNP MPs (Members of Parliament) elected since 1997; SNP MSPs (Members of the Scottish Parliament) elected since 1999; SNP MEPs (Members of the European Parliament) elected since 1999; members of the SNP National Executive Committee (NEC) including national office-bearers since 1997 (as defined by the party's constitution). There was considerable overlap between these groups.

Interviews were semi-structured and focused on three key themes: party organization; political strategy; and perceptions of nationalism and ideology. The first task of the interviews was to assess perceptions of power within the SNP. Interviewees were asked to consider the role of party elites in relation to different tiers within the organization, including ordinary members and party conferences. Questions relating to candidate and leadership selection and to the development of policy were examined in detail. In the area of political strategy, interviews explored opinion on the party's political programme, the party's relationship with other parties, and the party's electoral strategy. Interviews also explored views on the relationship between Scotland and Europe, what it means to be a nationalist and the political values associated with it, as well as the ideological cleavages within nationalism and perceptions of the relationship between nationalism and liberalism.

There are three main reasons to deploy both survey and in-depth interview methods (see Tashakkori and Teddlie, 1998; Read and Marsh, 2002). First, the different approaches are suited to addressing different research questions. A mass survey – as employed in membership studies – is the obvious means of collecting data on the demographic background, political attitudes, and behaviour of party members. Yet it is not suitable to explore issues of party organization and decision-making, which are generally addressed through elite interviews (e.g. Russell, 2005). Second, on some of our research questions – notably those concerning the role of members within the organization – it was useful to compare the perspectives of elites and members, to triangulate findings, and to highlight points of disagreement worthy of further investigation (Patton, 1990). Third, as Creswell (1994) describes, mixing methods in this way allows for an iterative process of asking and answering research questions. In particular, findings from a survey can guide data collection at the interview stage. For example, interviews can gauge the responses of the party elite to the preferences reported by members. In short, the combination of methods makes this study greater than the sum of its quantitative and qualitative parts.

2

From Blackmail to Governing Potential

Introduction

The Scottish National Party (SNP) formed the Scottish Government in May 2007 having become Scotland's largest party for the first time in its history (see Table 2.1). Its victory over Labour was narrow. The SNP won 47 seats in the 129 seat Scottish Parliament while Labour won 46, but the narrowness of victory masked a transformation in SNP fortunes over a short period of time. Prior to the establishment of the Scottish Parliament in 1999, the SNP had been a minor force in British politics. It was never Scotland's second party in terms of Parliamentary representation at Westminster. It was the second party in share of the

Table 2.1. Results of Scottish Parliament elections, 1999–2007

	Constituencies		Regional lists		Total	
	Votes (%)	Seats	Votes (%)	Seats	Seats	Seats (%)
1999						
Conservative	15.6	0	15.4	18	18	13.9
Labour	38.8	53	33.8	3	56	43.4
Liberal Democrats	14.2	12	12.5	5	17	13.2
SNP	28.7	7	27.0	28	35	27.1
Others	2.7	1	11.2	2	3	2.3
2003						
Conservative	16.6	3	15.6	15	18	13.9
Labour	34.6	46	29.4	4	50	38.8
Liberal Democrats	15.3	13	11.8	4	17	13.2
SNP	23.8	9	20.9	18	27	20.9
2007						
Conservative	16.6	4	13.9	13	17	13.2
Labour	32.2	37	29.2	9	46	35.7
Liberal Democrats	16.2	11	11.3	5	16	12.4
SNP	32.9	21	31.0	26	47	36.4
Others	2.1	0	14.6	3	3	2.4

vote on only two occasions before devolution: October 1974 and 1997. Since devolution, it held onto its position as second party in share of the vote in 2001 but fell behind the Liberal Democrats in 2005 but returned to second place in share of the vote in 2010. Devolution altered the opportunity structure for the SNP in two main ways. First, the Additional Member System (AMS) electoral system used for the Scottish Parliament translated votes into seats more favourably for the SNP. Compared with that of other parties, the SNP's support had traditionally been evenly spread across Scotland, leaving it unable to break through and win many constituency contests even when its vote rose. Though the party continued to struggle for first-past-the-post seats, it was compensated with regional list seats under AMS. Second, devolution created Scottish political space, distinct from UK politics, where the SNP was likely to be seen as more relevant. The familiar argument against a 'wasted vote' for third parties in Westminster elections, with the additional territorial dimension for the SNP given that it only contested about 10 per cent of Westminster seats, did not apply in elections to the Scottish Parliament.

These changes transformed the SNP's fortunes. Sartori (1976) suggested that parties had two sources of relevance: the potential to form a government; and the potential to blackmail, or affect the tactics of, governing parties. Devolution gave the SNP governing potential, in addition to the blackmail potential which it previously had. At the first Holyrood elections in 1999, the SNP became Scotland's second party, after Labour, both in terms of votes cast and seats won. The party's support dipped at the end of the first fixed four-year Parliament in 2003 but it still retained its position as Scotland's second party. While it had become a serious challenger for government office in Edinburgh, it remained marginal in Westminster.

Devolution not only represented a change in the electoral opportunity structure for the SNP but also altered the SNP as a party. Its six MPs elected at the 1997 UK election all stood as candidates in the first elections to the Scottish Parliament in 1999 and five of the six stood down from Westminster at the subsequent 2001 UK general election (the exception was Alex Salmond who, having stood down as leader of the SNP, decided to resign from Holyrood but remain an MP in 2001). This signalled the emphasis placed on the Scottish Parliament and its elections by the SNP. While six Labour MPs (out of fifty-six) and two Liberal Democrat MPs (out of ten) also stood for the Scottish Parliament (there were no Conservative Scottish MPs at the time), these were small proportions of their Scottish MPs. This focus had always been part of the SNP's core ideological make-up. A survey of Scottish MPs in the 1970s found that all but one of the SNP's eleven MPs had intended to stand for the Scottish Assembly which was then proposed, compared with only 21 per cent of Labour and 9 per cent of Conservative MPs in Scotland at the time (Mishler and Mughan, 1978: 400). However, while devolution was the single most significant event affecting the SNP in its history, it did not result in a complete break with the past. Devolution no more offered the SNP a 'Year Zero' than it did any other institution in Scotland (Mitchell, 2009a: 13). While it created new opportunities, adjustments were necessary and these were not always painless. This involved significant organizational and internal constitutional change, a shift in the locus of power (even if the same individuals remained the key players), and dealing with the legacy of earlier internal tensions. In this chapter, the SNP's internal politics pre-devolution and in devolution's early years are discussed. Debates about the kind of political party it should be both organizationally and ideologically, the pressures of being a largely extra-Parliamentary party and the nature of internal tensions are all considered.

Compromising unity

All political parties are broad churches. As Oliver Brown, a leading post-war Scottish Nationalist put it, 'I bitterly regret the day I compromised the unity of my party by admitting the second member' (Brown, 1969: 86). Beller and Belloni listed causes of factionalism within parties to include:

> sociological complexity of the party; ideological looseness of the party; the origin of the party in a merger of predecessor parties; the party's internal looseness or decentralized structure, especially a caucus-type party structure; and most important, the use of proportional representation for intraparty representation in elective party assemblies and executive bodies. (Beller and Belloni, 1978: 435)

These were all evident in the SNP at its foundation and for most of its history. The SNP came into being as the result of two parties merging in 1934: the National Party of Scotland (NPS), which had been set up in 1928; and the Scottish Party, styled the 'Moderates', which had been set up in 1932. The NPS had been set up after the failure of a series of home rule bills in the 1920s and disillusionment with established parties, especially Labour (Finlay, 1994). The Scottish Party was established as an alternative nationalist party by more conventional forces in Scottish society and politics who viewed the NPS as separatist and too left-wing.

From the outset, the choice was less about whether the SNP should be left- or right-wing, which would have been resolved in favour of being on the left simply through force of numbers, but rather about whether it should appeal across social classes to the nation as a whole or whether it should tailor its appeal to the working classes or at least progressive forces. While one view held that it was necessary to avoid being a single-issue party and required policies on a broad range of issues, another view was that the party should seek to maximize its support by avoiding placing itself firmly on the left–right spectrum. At times, this manifested itself in a debate as to whether the SNP should be a party or a movement. Those who saw the SNP as a party, as opposed to a movement organization, argued that it needed to develop a range of policies beyond simply advocating self-government. As McAllister has pointed out, this had two dimensions: 'whether to organize in a distinctive *differentiated organization*, or to rely on *communal permeation*' and 'whether to pursue their aims *electorally*, by nominating candidates cross-locally for public office throughout the country, or *non-electorally*, by utilizing a strategy other than electoral competition' (McAllister, 1981: 238). The differentiated organization strategy involved supporters pursuing goals through organizations specifically set up for the purpose while communal penetration involved supporters penetrating other existing organizations in pursuit of the goal. These questions give rise to four options (Figure 2.1). At various stages, the SNP has been an organization with characteristics of each of these options, apart from those of the entryist category. As a party with no prospect of forming a government at Westminster but with blackmail potential, it operated simultaneously as a party and pressure group. At times when it had difficulty in contesting elections, it operated as part of the wider national movement in Scotland and sought to set the agenda of other parties.

During its first fourteen years, it was possible to be a member of the SNP and another party. Even one of its leaders had dual membership in this period. Douglas Young had been a Labour Party member until he

	DIFFERENTIATED ORGANIZATION	COMMUNAL PERMEATION
ELECTORAL	Political Party	Entryist Group
NON-ELECTORAL	Pressure Group Protest Group	Social Movement Social Category

Figure 2.1. Party organization typology

Source: McAllister (1981: 239).

became SNP chairman in 1942 and argued against efforts to ban dual membership when this was proposed over the next few years. In 1943, the SNP voted to prevent office-bearers belonging to other parties and in 1948 the SNP's annual conference then extended prohibition on dual membership to the entire party. Young resigned when it became clear that this would be enforced. He argued that the party should remain as it had begun, 'organisationally independent of other political parties, while welcoming individual members of any or all of them for particular objectives, electoral and other' (Somerville, 2009: 28). It was, as Robert Crawford, a former SNP research officer, remarked, the 'final act in a drama which saw the SNP being transformed from a mere movement into the form, if not the substance, of a mass political party' (Crawford, 1982: 66). Crawford's comment on the lack of substance is a useful reminder that for much of its history the SNP was a tiny fringe organization with very few members.

Though one of the reasons for having an independent party was to contest elections, a view remained that the party ought to operate as a pressure group trying to influence the main parties. In the late 1940s, Roland Muirhead, one of its leading members (and funders), left to set up the Scottish National Congress believing that direct action, rather than electoral politics, was the way forward. From then on, the issue was less whether the party *should* but whether it *could* contest elections, and there were occasions when the SNP stood aside, usually because of lack of resources or as part of some potential electoral pact. The most notable case of the latter came in 1965 when the SNP decided not to stand against Liberal candidate David Steel in a by-election in Scottish Borders. The SNP had then been attempting to negotiate an electoral pact with the Liberals.

However, even had it gained significant levels of public support, the SNP had no governing potential as it contested elections only in Scotland. The SNP's relevance lay in its blackmail potential but this would be realized only if it advanced electorally. That created internal tensions. Concerns were frequently expressed that failure to contest elections undermined its *raison d'être* but there were also concerns that poor electoral performances would undermine its objectives (Halliday, 2011). Underlying these debates was the question of whether the SNP existed to put pressure on the existing parties, particularly Labour, or whether it could realistically expect to bring about its goals on its own. The SNP's relationship with other parties and political movements was a source of much internal debate. Throughout its existence, the party wrestled with whether and, if so, how it should work with other parties and organizations in Scotland.

Organization and ethos

As Crawford noted, the SNP as a political party might be dated from 1948 when the decision was taken to make membership of any other party incompatible with SNP membership. A basic structure was created that remained largely in place for fifty years. While there was disagreement on the precise definition of the party's goals and strategy, two central elements of the party's ethos are discernible and influenced its structure and constitution: decentralization and participation.

According to a survey of SNP local leaders in the late 1960s, the single most distinguishing feature of the party other than its support for self-government was that it was more democratically organized and responsive to local needs and pressures (Schwarz, 1970: 498). There were two main reasons for SNP support for decentralization. In common with other grass-roots movements, decentralization and participation involved both an organizational form and an ideological commitment. These were facets which would later be associated with new social movements. Melucci's comment on new social movements is apposite in the case of the SNP over most of its history, 'the new organizational form of contemporary movements is not just instrumental for their goals. It is a goal in itself' (Melucci, 1984: 830). First, there was an ideological commitment. Self-government rather than independence was the party's stated goal and this was interpreted as involving decentralization and participation. This was reflected in the internal structures of the party as well as in the party's manifestos and public policies. Second, the SNP was an extra-Parliamentary party for much of its history. It relied heavily on activism at a local level. Additionally, until 1999, the Parliamentary party was not only small but hostile to the institution to which it was elected. The party's goal was to break with Westminster, not to form a government there. The consequence of being an extra-Parliamentary party with a weak financial base was that it was an almost entirely voluntary party. Party duties and responsibilities had to be spread amongst its leaders who were in full-time employment outside politics.

This ethos took shape in a number of organizational forms. The party had little faith in leaders. Indeed, the party had no formal leader but instead had a 'Chairman', latterly referred to as Convener, until 2004. This was more than a matter of terminology. Party activists jealously guarded against efforts to extend the Chairman/Convener's role beyond that of chairing the party. Even when it had eleven MPs in the late 1970s, the SNP's National Chairman was outside Parliament, indeed someone who had a full-time job outside politics. In addition to the National Chairman, the 1948 constitution allowed for two Vice Chairmen. Over time, the number of Vice Chairmen/Conveners grew. As its membership and support grew, but without the concomitant increase in MPs, the SNP was forced to create more senior office-bearers to deal with the increased burden of a growing extra-Parliamentary party.

Amongst the many constraints imposed on the National Convener was the SNP's annual conference, described in its 1948 constitution as the 'supreme governing body of the Party' (Brand, 1978: 306). The annual conference, consisting of branch and constituency delegates, was the key decision-making body of the party. Branches of the party were invested with considerable power and had the right to propose resolutions and nominate members for national office. This meant that any SNP branch could nominate *any* party member for national office including National Convener. This could result in a challenge each year to an incumbent national office-holder from a tiny number of discontented party members, though challenges rarely happened.

Mansbach (1973) maintained that this decentralized structure and ethos inhibited the SNP in mobilizing voters on a national basis:

> The lack of discipline, the democratic mode of election to high party office, the decentralized direction and lack of coordination of party affairs, and the localist concerns and attitudes of branch leaders prepared the party to compete successfully in local contests and by-elections but not to mobilize for a General Election. The very organizational attributes of the party which facilitated the attraction of new members, particularly outside Scotland's urban centers, make it more difficult for the SNP to compete successfully in a General Election. (Mansbach, 1973: 197)

However, decentralization was the party's *raison d'être* and its local activists provided it with its energy and drive. It also meant that local branches had autonomy to make policy suitable to local communities, helping the party in local elections in the late 1960s.

Electoral success had an impact on the party's structures. Crawford argued that, from 1948 until 1962, the SNP was organizationally more devolved and less oligarchic than thereafter (Crawford, 1982: 64). The SNP started its slow advance around 1962 and a new generation of leaders emerged principally around Billy Wolfe, later to become SNP National Chairman (1969–79). A number of key figures who joined at this time and had considerable influence brought what today would be referred to as 'New Politics' (Poguntke, 1993: 10), then described as

'New Left' ideas, into the SNP. Amongst these members were some who were actively engaged in establishing workers' cooperatives and who were deeply involved in campaigning for unilateral nuclear disarmament. This same group was amongst the leading environmentalists in the SNP in the 1970s, establishing the party's long-standing opposition to nuclear energy, nuclear waste dumping, and support for alternative energy sources.

Wolfe had been relatively unknown in the SNP prior to standing as SNP candidate in the 1962 West Lothian by-election. He later recalled how he started his climb through the ranks of the party after the by-election when he came second with 23 per cent of the vote:

> Although unknown to all but two of the persons attending that Council meeting [following the by-election], apart from being the man who had 9,750 votes in West Lothian, I was appointed Convener of the Party's Economics Committee, a member of the Party's National Executive Committee, and a member of the Election Committee which is responsible for interviewing and assessing the members nominated as possible Parliamentary candidates; and I was authorized to issue statements to the Press on the subject of the Scottish economy. (Wolfe, 1973: 18)

Gordon Wilson, Wolfe's successor as National Chairman (1979–90), records a similar experience of rapid promotion around the same time (Wilson, 2009: 6). Opportunities to hold national office within the party were in inverse proportion to opportunities to hold public office.

In 1963, the SNP set up an enquiry under Wilson into its organization and structure. Wilson concluded that it was the 'absence of direction which plagued the SNP in the post-war period' (Crawford, 1982: 87). He proposed a structure that would remain in place, changing only incrementally, until 2004. Power shifted to the National Chairman and National Executive Committee from the larger national council. Though there was still no appetite for a leader, there was less ambiguity than previously with the party chairman becoming the accepted political head of the party and the position of party presidency established as an honorific post. According to Crawford, the election of executive Vice Chairmen (later Vice Conveners and increasing in number from two in 1964 to six by 2004) 'truly represented the major advance towards a centralised structure' (Ibid.: 140). However, it was centralized compared only to what had gone before. The SNP remained a highly decentralized party compared with electorally successful parties in Scotland. An effort to centralize the party's finances, for example, was rejected. Branches retained control of the money they raised, including membership fees, only making a contribution to party headquarters.

McAllister's study of party organization and minority nationalism noted that none of the three constitutional nationalist parties in the United Kingdom – SNP, Plaid Cymru (PC), and Northern Ireland's Social Democratic and Labour Party (SDLP) – 'possessed a cohesive party organization prior to the 1960s' but that, by the 1970 general election, each had become 'increasingly professional, gauged by the staff employed' marking a 'shift from amateurism to professionalism' (McAllister, 1981: 240–1). However, this professionalism operated alongside the continuation of its highly decentralized structure and depended on income generated from influxes of members following electoral advances. This made it unstable. Ultimately, the SNP relied heavily on a core of figures who were not engaged in full-time politics. This structure may have made sense so long as the party was largely an extra-Parliamentary body, relying heavily on volunteers and campaigning for self-government. It would make less sense once it became a party seriously competing for governmental power under devolution. The strengths that decentralization and participation, voluntarism and branch power gave the SNP prior to 1999 would become impediments to progress thereafter.

The main reason these were the dominant characteristics of the SNP was lack of resources. The party had no corporate supporters of the sort that Labour and Conservative Parties had. It relied on small individual donations though periodically it attracted larger donations and legacies. The film star Sean Connery became the SNP's main donor in the years immediately before devolution. Occasionally, it received significant legacies left in wills but its finances fluctuated from year-to-year dependent on its media profile and electoral performance. The test of the depth of the party's commitment to decentralization and participation would come in the new era of devolution.

Ideology of the SNP

The central element of the SNP's doctrine has been self-government though its precise meaning and how it was to be achieved were disputed. Whether self-government amounts to independence or some measure of home rule short of independence was a central doctrinal dispute in its formative years. These differences were evident at the outset. The NPS constitution resolved this tension with a compromise:

Self-government for Scotland with independent national status within the British group of nations, together with the reconstruction of Scottish National Life. (quoted in Brand, 1978: 302)

The party's 1948 constitution edged it closer to a more radical objective though 'independence' was still not mentioned:

Self-government for Scotland. The restoration of Scottish national sovereignty by the establishment of a democratic Scottish government whose authority will be limited only by such agreements as will be freely entered into with other nations in order to further international co-operation and world peace. (quoted in Ibid.: 302)

One senior party member who had joined in the early 1960s, who was interviewed for this study, noted that 'home rule' was the term most often used by the party to describe its aims at that time. Independence became the rallying cry later. Ideological disputes were then replaced by strategic tensions over the party's attitude to devolution, whether it was a stepping stone to independence or would block progress to that end.

Sovereignty became a shibboleth in nationalist circles. The idea of Scottish popular sovereignty assumed symbolic importance to the SNP following the Royal Titles legal case in 1953. John MacCormick, a founding member of the SNP who had left the party in 1942 to set up a home rule pressure group, contested the right of the monarch to be styled Elizabeth II on the grounds that the first Elizabeth had not been Queen of Scotland. The case was lost but not before the Lord President of the Court of Session, Scotland's most senior judge, had given his opinion that 'the principle of unlimited sovereignty of Parliament is a distinctively English principle and has no counterpart in Scottish constitutional law' (MacCormick, 1955: 216). The contrast between Scottish notions of popular sovereignty and English notions of Parliamentary sovereignty may have seemed abstruse to some commentators (Levy, 1990: 70) but is central to any understanding of the SNP in this period. At its core, the SNP's late twentieth-century Scottish nationalism espoused the view that the Scottish people should determine Scotland's political and constitutional future rather than Parliament at Westminster. At its heart lay a different conception of the state's relationship with its citizens. Indeed, the idea of 'subjects of the Crown' was anathema to the SNP though this did not necessarily lead to rejection of constitutional monarchy.

The most significant tension within the SNP was that between what came to be called its fundamentalist and pragmatic wings, that is, between those who upheld the party's fundamental objectives and those willing to compromise in favour of electoral advance. Beer noted the battle between fundamentalism and revisionism in the Labour Party in the 1950s. Labour's revisionists advocated a 'degree of adaptation of policy in view of governmental and electoral problems confronting the party' (Beer, 1982: 219). Fundamentalists in the SNP were initially described as those who 'identify with the "independence – nothing less" position and wary of the party becoming too closely associated with a position on the left–right axis' (Mitchell, 1988: 743). The alternative position in the SNP was not so much revisionist, as this suggests revising the party's central doctrinal position. The SNP's pragmatic wing appeared as committed to independence as its fundamentalists but differed in the route to be taken. The differences may have been strategic rather than ideological but were no less important.

One of the most important debates on strategy came at the party's annual conference in Motherwell in 1976. The SNP then decided that it was 'prepared to accept an assembly with limited powers as a possible stepping stone' (SNP, 1976). However, almost 40 per cent of delegates rejected this, provoking Billy Wolfe, party chairman, to warn his party later in the year, 'We must avoid projecting an aggressive or destructive image...It is safer to risk provoking impatience among our dedicated supporters than to try to satisfy nationalist sentiment at the risk of alienating new support' (Wolfe, 1976). For the most part, those sceptical of the devolutionary path to independence were willing to accept this pragmatism at that time.

In addition to self-government, the SNP has always specified a further aim in its constitution, a point made by a number of those interviewed. The SNP's 2004 constitution refers to the 'furtherance of all Scottish interests' (SNP constitution 2004a: para. 2b). The vagueness of this aim may explain why it has been largely ignored in commentaries. However, the interpretation of this second objective has been as much disputed internally and is almost as central to the development of the SNP as 'self-government'. The 'furtherance of all Scottish interests' became a debate between left and right. Did it mean supporting nationalization or privatization, supporting state education or private education, redistribution of wealth or allowing the free market to allocate wealth? The SNP contained a broad spectrum of views and this inevitably gave rise to tensions. While support for self-government might have united the party, there were tensions as to the kind of self-governing Scotland that SNP members wanted.

A key issue for the SNP has been the relationship between its two aims, whether it should prioritize pursuing self-government or policies beneficial to Scotland. As well as a tension on the meaning of self-government, there were tensions on whether to support devolution as a stepping stone or view it with suspicion – 'independence nothing less' – and whether its constitutional goal should be pursued to the exclusion of all else – 'independence – nothing else'. The perception that the SNP was a single-issue party and needed to develop a series of policies and establish a coherent position on the conventional left–right spectrum led to a period of policymaking led by Billy Wolfe and associates in the 1960s and 1970s. An element in the SNP feared that the focus on policymaking detracted from campaigning for its primary goal of self-government, however defined, especially when the party had little prospect of forming a government but as SNP members were elected as councillors and MPs, the need for policies became more obvious.

From fringe to breakthrough

Prior to devolution, the SNP's Parliamentary presence had been precarious (Table 2.2). Robert McIntyre, its first MP, was elected in a by-election in the closing weeks of the Second World War when a wartime truce between the main parties still operated. This electoral truce meant that

Table 2.2. SNP candidates and share of vote in UK general elections

Election	Candidates	Lost deposits	Share of Scottish vote (%)	Mean vote in seats contested (%)	Seats
1929	2	2	0.1	5.2	0
1931	5	2	1.0	12.3	0
1935	8	5	1.3	12.2	0
1945	8	6	1.2	9.4	0
1950	3	3	0.4	7.4	0
1951	2	1	0.3	19.9	0
1955	2	1	0.5	14.7	0
1959	5	3	0.8	11.3	0
1964	15	12	2.4	10.6	0
1966	23	10	5.0	14.1	0
1970	65	43	11.4	12.8	1
1974 (Feb)	70	7	21.9	22.1	7
1974 (Oct)	71	0	30.4	30.4	11
1979	71	29	17.3	17.3	2
1983	72	53	11.8	11.8	2
1987	71	1	14.0	14.1	3
1992	72	0	21.5	21.5	3
1997	72	0	21.9	21.9	6
2001	72	0	21.1	21.1	5
2005	59	0	17.7	17.7	6
2010	59	0	19.9	19.9	6

by-elections were fought only by the party that had previously held the seat. The SNP was not party to the agreement and, like Common Wealth elsewhere in Britain, was a beneficiary. The truce ended when the 1945 general election was called three months later and McIntyre lost the seat. Agitation for a Scottish Parliament was at its peak in the immediate post-war period, partly in response to perceptions that the Attlee Government's programme was centralizing power and undermining Scottish institutions, but the SNP had a peripheral role and this activity died away by the early 1950s. After a split in 1942, some of the key figures from its foundation left the party to campaign within a cross-party pressure group for a Parliament short of independence but this campaign fizzled out by the early 1950s.

From then until the 1960s, success for the SNP was measured in the number of candidates it was able to field and proportion of saved deposits. It struggled even by these modest standards. For many years, the party's very existence was uncertain. As Hanham (1969: 179) remarked, the 'great achievement of the SNP from 1942 to 1964 was simply to have survived'. According to a former senior party member from this time, the SNP had about 200 members in the late 1950s. It is tempting, but ahistorical, to view the SNP's development from the fringe of politics to government as a gradual process of growing relevance. There was nothing inevitable about the SNP's progress to power. Political history is littered with long forgotten parties that failed to gain relevance and there were many occasions when the SNP came close to being one. In 1959, the *Glasgow Herald* wrote the obituary of Scottish nationalism (*Glasgow Herald*, 8 and 9 July 1959). It was wrong but few thought so at the time including some within the SNP.

Not for the last time, however, an SNP obituary was followed by a revival. A series of improvements in SNP performance in local elections and by-elections in the early 1960s presaged a breakthrough when Winnie Ewing won the Hamilton by-election in November 1967. There remains debate about why the SNP did well in this period. Some explanations focus on the changing environment in which the SNP operated including the unpopularity of the Labour Government at that time (Webb and Hall, 1978). Others suggested that 'alienation from the existing British political system' was relevant (Brand, 1978: 293). Others still focus on the more professional approach adopted by the SNP (Harvie, 2004: 168). The likelihood is that each set of explanations is relevant.

The immediate impact of Ewing's election was an increased focus on Scottish affairs in Westminster and Whitehall (Mitchell, 2009a: 112). The SNP's blackmail potential was evident. The Labour Government established a Royal Commission on the Constitution to examine devolution and Edward Heath, leader of the Conservative Party, announced a change in his party's policy in favour of a modest measure of devolution. There was considerable media interest in and, for a period, even some media sympathy for the party. SNP membership soared. The party had about 300 branches in September 1967 increasing to 420 within 8 months. SNP Headquarters had a fairly good idea of how many branches it had as these had to be registered but, as Gordon Wilson recalled, 'SNP membership figures could be difficult to gauge, largely because the party was decentralised with cards being sold at local level. Branches were very poor at sending records of members to HQ' (Wilson, 2009: 40). Estimates of around 120,000 members were made. One academic study at the time seemed to confirm this figure on the basis of surveying 18 per cent of SNP branches (Mansbach, 1973: 185). Given that the SNP had only polled 128,474 votes at the 1966 election (contesting twenty-three of Scotland's seventy-one seats), this would have been a staggering increase in membership. It is now widely accepted within the SNP, and acknowledged in interviews with senior party members from that time, that this was inaccurate. Gordon Wilson and others from that time now suggest that it was more likely to have been between 60,000 and 70,000.

Another idea that developed at this time, though one with stronger foundations, was that the SNP was a party attractive to young people. In the late 1960s, the SNP's electoral breakthrough resulted in some serious empirical research of the party's demographic profile and ideological outlook. Schwarz (1970: 496) found that, while 79 per cent of Labour and Conservative local leaders were above 37 years of age, this was true of only 43 per cent of SNP local leaders. This age profile was confirmed in another study. Mansbach found that between 1967 and 1969, the average age of SNP national office-bearers and candidates for national office was 37.5. The average ages of selected Parliamentary candidates and Council candidates in Glasgow were 39.5 and 36.9, respectively.

The Schwarz study also found that SNP local leaders had a strong Scottish identity compared with Conservative and Labour local party leaders (Schwarz, 1970: 512). Hanham's study of Scottish nationalism referred to the 'television maintenance man and the fitter snatched away from their workshops' being 'no substitute for an experienced local leadership' in describing the SNP of the late 1960s (Hanham, 1969: 179–80). However, research offered a different picture. SNP local leaders had been active in 'intermediary groups' – pressure groups and professional, trade or technical associations – and there was little empirical evidence to back claims that the SNP attracted the kind of Poujadist tendencies that its opponents claimed (Schwarz, 1970: 504). SNP members felt economically secure and felt that they personally had satisfying prospects whatever they thought of Scotland's prospects under the union. Mansbach (1973) confirmed that its local leaders were rooted in local communities. Local roots combined with uneven growth and 'opposition to "giantism" and centralization' (Mansbach, 1973: 188) to present the SNP as a 'representative of Scottish communal feeling' (Ibid.). The party had benefitted from a 'more traditional short-term negativism toward the Government in Westminster' (Ibid.) in urban Scotland but its deeper roots elsewhere limited its appeal to more sparsely populated areas over the longer term.

The SNP itself conducted a survey of its activists in 1970 and found that 70 per cent saw achieving 'self-government' as its primary objective with 24 per cent seeing 'reformist rule' and 'social reform' as primary to its objectives (Crawford, 1982: 4). At a stage when class consciousness was much higher than today, 80 per cent of SNP activists did not identify with any class and 78 per cent had never previously been members of any other party (Ibid.).

SNP in Westminster

Winnie Ewing lost Hamilton at the 1970 general election. However, the SNP won the Western Isles in that election, the first seat it had won in a general election. It contested sixty-five out of seventy-one Scottish seats and won 11.4 per cent of the vote, its best result to date but, measured against the hype, it was seen as a setback. A constant theme of SNP campaigns over many elections has been unrealistic expectations. The 1970 election result suggested that the SNP had been a 'flash party' (Converse and Dupeux, 1962; Rose and Mackie, 1988) based on protest votes (McLean, 1970). Once more, SNP obituaries were followed by growth in support for the party. In November 1973, a by-election in Glasgow Govan saw the SNP regain the initiative. While the party lost Govan in the general election three months later, it held the Western Isles and gained an additional six seats. Seven months later, in the October 1974 election, the SNP won eleven seats with 30 per cent of the vote, coming only 6 percentage points behind Labour though winning thirty fewer Scottish seats (Table 2.3).

There are a number of explanations for the SNP successes in 1974. The SNP's rise fitted with British-wide explanations focused on class and partisan dealignment (Crewe et al., 1977). Parties such as the SNP had more success in appealing to voters who were becoming detached from established parties. The United Kingdom, as indeed other advanced

Table 2.3. Scottish vote and seats in Westminster elections, 1970–2010

Seats	SNP seats	vote (%)	Labour	vote (%)	Conservative	vote (%)	Liberal/Alliance/ Liberal Democrat	vote (%)
1970	1	11.4	44	44.5	23	38.0	3	5.5
1974 (Feb)	7	21.9	40	36.6	21	32.9	3	8.0
1974 (Oct)	11	30.4	41	36.3	16	24.7	3	8.3
1979	2	17.3	44	41.5	22	31.4	3	9.0
1983	2	11.8	43	35.1	21	28.4	8	24.5
1987	3	14.0	50	42.4	10	24.0	9	19.2
1992	3	21.5	49	39.0	11	25.6	9	13.1
1997	6	22.1	56	45.6	0	17.5	10	13.0
2001	5	20.1	55	43.3	1	15.6	10	16.4
2005	6	17.7	40	38.9	1	15.8	11	22.6
2010	6	19.9	41	42.0	1	16.7	11	18.9

liberal democracies, was in economic crisis caused in part by the quadrupling of oil prices in the Middle East. The SNP had an immediate response with the discovery of North Sea oil. Its slogan, 'It's Scotland's oil' gave the party relevance even though research suggests that it was less significant than is generally imagined in improving SNP fortunes. The main study of the 1974 election in Scotland concluded that SNP support was closely related to support for devolution and independence, and that young people were more inclined to support devolution (Miller, 1981: 226). Oil was far less important than constitutional preference in directly explaining SNP support though the discovery of oil may have affected constitutional preference.

As the SNP became an electoral force, albeit with a precarious Parliamentary presence, it needed a policy profile. A study of the SNP in the 1970 election had described it as 'something of a "Social-Democratic" party, rather more collectivist than the Liberals, yet apparently opposed to centralization and bureaucracy' (Kellas, 1971: 457). In its February 1974 election manifesto, the SNP explicitly referred to the 'programme of social democracy which the Scottish National Party proposes for the foundations of a self-governing Scotland' (SNP, 1974: 5). In the 1974–79 Parliament, the SNP had eleven MPs and this group's voting record was scrutinized by the media and its opponents to see whether it voted more often with the Labour Government or the Conservative Opposition (Table 2.4). This would be the first time a group of SNP members was scrutinized carefully. These MPs hardly knew each other before being elected but needed to cohere as a group. The MPs were 'not necessarily united on policy matters and frequently took decisions by narrow votes'

Table 2.4. SNP MPs voting behaviour, 1974–79

	With Government (%)	With Conservatives (%)	With others only (%)	Free votes (%)
6 March–31 July 1974	66.2	21.6	6.8	5.4
1974/75	37.7	49	10.9	2.3
1975/76	35.4	45.6	7.7	11.4
1976/77	37.0	43.0	10.9	9.1
1977/78	63.2	17.3	11.7	7.9
1978/79	46.7	20	18.3	15

Source: Wilson (2009).

according to one of them (Wilson, 2009: 119). Outwardly, it looked as if an even greater tension existed between the MPs and National Executive Committee (NEC) members. There was a perception amongst sections of the SNP in Glasgow and urban Scotland that the MPs, representing largely rural areas, projected an image that was unhelpful in urban Scotland. Retrospectively, Wilson suggests that the real source of tension arose from a 'muddle in party strategy' as the SNP 'oscillated between devolution as against independence and devolution against economic issues' (Ibid.: 165), that is, debating whether it should adopt a pragmatic versus fundamentalist approach and whether it should emphasize constitutional or economic issues. In a paper written after the 1979 election, Billy Wolfe identified a series of problems that had undermined the SNP, 'What I believe the Parliamentary group have wittingly or unwittingly reduced us to is a fundamentalist nationalist image. We have lost the social-democratic middle ground, and both of the main parties can point to us and say that we are either anti-Tory or anti-Labour' (Wolfe, 1979). Wolfe identified a number of causes for the party's decline: the behaviour of its MPs; the abandonment of its social democratic image; and poor relations between the MPs and executive. The SNP suffered from the lack of clear leadership whether caused by a split leadership structure, strategic, and ideological incoherence, or both. The group of MPs took a different view, seeing some members of the NEC undermining their work, unable to appreciate constituency pressures and the need to take a stance on a range of Parliamentary votes on a daily basis.

During the 1974–79 Parliament, the SNP kept a record of how its MPs voted in the Commons. Despite building an anti-Tory coalition of support that allowed it to take nine seats from the Conservatives, the SNP's MPs were keen to show that they were independent of both main parties. The SNP group kept the minority Labour Government in power towards the end of the 1974–79 Parliament but withdrew that support when Labour failed to push ahead with its devolution legislation following the 1979 referendum. Contrary to early polls suggesting that there was a convincing majority for devolution, the result was a very narrow victory in favour of devolution but insufficient to overcome the weighted majority that had been set by Westminster. It was a serious blow to the pragmatists in the SNP. Having given fulsome support for the Yes side in the devolution referendum, the SNP was associated with the defeat.

SNP support peaked in early 1976 and the party failed to live up to expectations in three successive by-elections in 1978, their struggles culminating in the loss of nine of its eleven seats and a loss of a third of its vote in the 1979 general election. The election came shortly after the referendum. The combination of defeat in the referendum and the loss of support at the general election had a devastating effect on the SNP. Despite this, SNP membership grew by 6 per cent in 1979–80, probably accounted for by by-election activity in May 1979, but it fell sharply in 1981 after the start of serious party infighting (Wilson, 2009: 206).

The shadow of 1979

In common with other parties that have suffered a major electoral defeat following a period of high expectations, the SNP turned on itself in 1979. From 1979 to 1983, it was riven by factional politics focused on what had gone wrong. One reaction was that the party needed to cut out a clearer position on the left–right axis while another was that the SNP needed to emphasize its support for independence, viewing its support for devolution in the 1979 referendum as a Labour trap. In Summer 1979, a group was set up, called the '79 Group'. Its membership largely consisted of younger SNP members and included deputy leader Margo MacDonald as well as Alex Salmond and Kenny MacAskill – both later to be members of the first SNP Government elected in 2007. Stephen Maxwell, one of the Group's leading figures, later argued that it was the younger element that tended to determine the Group's tactics (Maxwell, 1985). The Group eased former Labour MP Jim Sillars's transition into the SNP but it was bitterly opposed by the SNP's two remaining MPs and Winnie Ewing, who won a seat in the first directly elected European Parliament elections in June 1979, as well as most of the party's old guard. The Group adopted three aims: independence; socialism; and republicanism. However, not all of its members signed up to these objectives. Some, including Salmond, preferred the vaguer aim of ensuring that the SNP cut out a clear position as a left of centre party. The SNP conference in Autumn 1979 was a raucous affair though there were few policy disputes. Although the party overwhelmingly backed calls for greater redistribution of wealth and opposition to nuclear weapons, there was no consensus on how its policy profile ought to be presented. Attitudes to devolution proved the most divisive issue on the conference agenda. A large majority supported a resolution stating that it should 'not engage in any more dealings in assemblies, devolution, or meaningful talks' (SNP, 1979: resolution 41). Gordon Wilson was elected leader, having tapped into the party's reaction against devolution. Although he had supported the pro-devolution strategy, he was much less closely associated with it than the other contender for the post, Stephen Maxwell, who had been in charge of the SNP's campaign for devolution in the 1979 referendum and was a leading figure in the 79 Group.

The party also dabbled with civil disobedience. At its 1981 conference, the party supported resolutions criticizing the 'failure of the private sector in Scotland' and called for an enlarged public sector and a 'real Scottish resistance' in defence of jobs involving direct action 'up to and including political strikes and civil disobedience on a mass scale'. There was support for 'armed neutrality' and opposition to NATO membership (SNP, 1981: resolutions 3, 17, and 36) at the conference. Jim Sillars was elected an SNP National Vice Chair and Alex Salmond was elected to the NEC for the first time. It was the 79 Group's apogee. The following year, the Campaign for Nationalism was established with a view to challenging the 79 Group. Most damagingly, the 79 Group became associated with the failed civil disobedience campaign after Sillars and five members of the Group were arrested for breaking into the building that had been intended to house the Scottish Assembly (Mitchell, 1996: 226–8). This led to Wilson successfully proposing the proscription of internal groups at the party's 1982 conference. In an interview, one of its leading members informed us that at its dissolution, the 79 Group had only 217 members but these included some of the party's most talented figures. The Group was disbanded but some of its members set up the Scottish Socialist Society (SSS), open to members of all parties in an effort to get around proscription. Margo MacDonald announced her resignation from the SNP and seven other members were expelled, including Alex Salmond and Kenny MacAskill, for being members of the executive of the SSS. The expulsions, subsequently commuted to suspensions, dominated internal SNP politics in the run-up to the 1983 general election.

Kenny MacAskill was the only suspended member to stand as an SNP candidate in the election.

The SNP held its two Westminster seats in 1983 though its vote fell by almost a third and it lost fifty-three out of seventy-two deposits. Its insecure position as a Parliamentary party was again highlighted at the 1987 election. Despite winning three new seats – in areas which had returned SNP MPs in the 1970s – it lost both of the seats it had previously held. Gordon Wilson, party leader, lost his seat in Dundee East having been MP since 1974 and the Western Isles returned a Labour Member for the first time since 1966. Though Wilson continued as party leader, the focus of media attention was on the new MPs and in particular on Alex Salmond, the MP for Banff and Buchan, who was elected Senior Vice Convener (deputy leader) at the 1987 SNP conference. Former Labour MP Jim Sillars took the Glasgow Govan seat for the SNP in a by-election in November 1988 and Dick Douglas, a disaffected Labour MP, defected to the SNP giving the party five seats when Parliament was dissolved in 1992. Both former Labour MPs were defeated at the 1992 election and the SNP was once more down to three seats though with a much improved vote. In 1997, the SNP gained much less than Labour from the Conservative wipe-out in Scotland and, though the Nationalists won six seats, they did so with only a very small increase (of 0.6 percentage points) in their vote share.

Towards the end of the 1979–83 Parliament, Gordon Wilson had adopted the label 'moderate left of centre' to describe the SNP. What was meant by 'left of centre' was unclear but it allowed consensus to emerge after years of internal divisions. More significant developments were intimated in August 1983 when Wilson initiated a number of reforms. He appointed an internal Commission that included Alex Salmond, John Swinney, and Alasdair Morgan to examine the party's organization. This would be the start of a long-standing working relationship between these three that would be important in internal SNP politics over the next quarter of a century. In addition, Wilson identified three policy areas where he sought changes: devolution; Europe; and defence. He feared the party was seen as outside the mainstream on each of these issues and especially needed to appear more in favour of devolution and the European Union (EU).

The SNP's image as a left-wing party was enhanced in the late 1980s through the election and prominence of Alex Salmond and Jim Sillars but more particularly through its support for civil disobedience in opposition to the poll tax. The party campaigned for non-payment of the tax. This campaign had a greater impact in changing the SNP's image than in stopping the poll tax. By the early 1990s, the SNP had established itself as being on the left of Scottish politics in the minds of the electorate (Bennie et al., 1997: 144). There was remarkable unity round this new position given that, only a few years before, Salmond and Sillars had been prominent members of the left-wing 79 Group and there had been strong opposition to their efforts to move the party to the left.

During the early 1980s, when the Campaign for Nuclear Disarmament was on the rise, the SNP hardened its opposition to nuclear weapons and came out against NATO membership. Wilson was keen that the SNP should abandon its opposition to NATO while maintaining its opposition to nuclear weapons. There was less support for Wilson's views on NATO and the party retained its opposition to membership. Successive leaders have left the issue alone. Significantly, many figures interviewed for this study emphasized the importance of unilateralism when giving reasons for joining the SNP. Senior members, whether associated with fundamentalism or gradualism, and whether on the left or right wings of the party, agree with the position. The SNP's deep-rooted opposition to nuclear weapons was summed up by one senior party figure who described opposition to nuclear weapons as being in the 'SNP's DNA'. This may explain why there have been few efforts to overturn opposition to NATO membership even though that alliance has many non-nuclear members.

Pragmatism re-asserted

In 1980, Wilson sponsored an unsuccessful Bill to create an elected Constitutional Convention to determine Scotland's constitutional status. He continued to argue for this and to soften the party's hard-line opposition to devolution. In his conference speech in 1983, Wilson acknowledged that independence gave the SNP its energy and dedication but warned that intransigence limited its appeal. Fundamentalism, he maintained, erected a barrier between the party and the electorate (*Scotsman*, 6 September 1983). At that conference, a resolution was passed confirming support for independence but which included the key phrase 'while in no way seeking to obstruct' devolution (SNP, 1983: resolution 22). Though the conference failed to support a Constitutional Convention, the party had softened its attitude to devolution. It moved hesitantly towards accepting devolution but with a core of dissenting voices. The most notable opponent was Jim Fairlie, deputy leader from 1981 to 1984, who had spoken against devolution at the 1976 Motherwell conference.

Over the next decade, the SNP edged further towards support for devolution. However, in the late 1980s, its hard-line image was reinforced when it refused to participate in a Constitutional Convention proposed by the cross-party pressure group Campaign for a Scottish Assembly (CSA). Agitation for home rule had been increasing against the backdrop of an unpopular Conservative Government with little support in Scotland. Labour and the Liberal Democrats, with the support of most local authorities, other smaller parties and a number of pressure groups, set up the Scottish Constitutional Convention. The Conservatives, as the party of government and deeply hostile to any form of devolution, refused to participate. The SNP was divided on whether to take part. SNP opponents of participation feared that the proposed composition of the Convention would result in Labour dominance. In March 1989, the SNP voted against participation after a heated debate at a meeting of its national council, its main decision-making body between annual conferences. The Convention drew up proposals for devolution which, in modified form, were eventually implemented. The SNP's failure to participate in the Convention meant that it was unable to shape devolution from within. However, the SNP had been important in shaping the political agenda. Rising support for the SNP, especially evident in the Glasgow Govan by-election in November 1989, strengthened Labour's commitment to devolution.

Once Labour was elected to government in 1997, the issue became whether the SNP would support devolution in the referendum later that year. By this stage, Alex Salmond had been leader for seven years and had been moving his party in that direction. An SNP National Council overwhelmingly supported a resolution reiterating 'primacy to the independence campaign, but which does not seek to obstruct devolution' and resolved to campaign for devolution including cooperating in a cross-party campaign (SNP, 1997). The lack of opposition from the SNP's hardliners has been explained by Alex Salmond's leadership skills, lessons learned from the experience of opposing devolution in the aftermath of the 1979 referendum, the backdrop of eighteen years of Conservative rule and the popularity of devolution in Scotland (Lynch, 2002: 222).

A similar softening process occurred on Europe. Wilson was aided in this because attitudes to devolution and particularly Europe cut across old divisions. Jim Sillars, Alex Salmond, and Kenny MacAskill – leading 79 Group members – all supported Wilson in his bid to shift the party to a more pro-European stance, as did Winnie Ewing, one of the leading critics of the Group. Once more, one of the key opponents of this shift was Jim Fairlie. Fairlie was joined by Isobel Lindsay, one of the leading supporters of devolution. Sovereignty was the basis of Fairlie's opposition to European integration and devolution. In a paper written for an internal debate in 1990, he defined the claim to sovereignty as a:

claim by some representative authority in the name of 'the people' to exercise a monopoly of law-making and law-enforcing within a designated territory. In an increasingly interdependent world sovereign states have accepted specific treaty limitations on their law-making rights. (Fairlie, 1990)

His objection was that the European Community, particularly the Single European Act, entailed an unacceptable 'surrender of Scottish national sovereignty' across many 'highly sensitive areas' (Ibid.). He argued that the new European policy was designed for two reasons: to undermine the 'separatist jibe'; and the 'Thatcher Factor', the latter suggesting that the SNP supported European integration because of Margaret Thatcher's Euro scepticism.

At its conference in 1988, the SNP supported a resolution by a margin of 8:1 advocating independence in Europe. Jim Sillars became the leading SNP figure articulating the case for 'independence in Europe' (Sillars, 1989, 1990). Sillars addressed sovereignty in his various contributions to the SNP's internal debates. He maintained that Scotland could not:

change fundamentally the policies which the Community developed and develops over the years before we become a member state in our own right ... it would be both unrealistic and politically dangerous to let loose the notion that we believe we can make the EC roll back from where it is when we reach the Council of Ministers. (Sillars, 1990)

In essence, the SNP's independence in Europe policy differed from its evolving pragmatism on devolution in that, while there may have been strategic electoral considerations involved in its attitude towards devolution, its European policy involved a significant revision of the party's understanding of independence. In late 1990, after over thirty years in the party, Jim Fairlie resigned from the SNP in opposition to this revisionism.

Conclusion

By the time of the first elections to the Scottish Parliament in 1999, the SNP had established itself as a pragmatic left of centre, pro-EU party. It perceived itself as more left-wing than Labour, a perception reinforced by Labour's shift to the centre ground under Tony Blair. Its most significant success during the period up to devolution was that it had survived. Beyond that, the SNP's most significant impact had been forcing the Scottish dimension onto the agenda of British politics and ultimately playing a central part in the creation of the Scottish Parliament. In each of these respects, it had been its blackmail role that had given it relevance. Under devolution, it would have a very different relevance as it would have the potential to become a party of government.

3

From Amateur-Activist to Electoral-Professional Party

Introduction

In his classic study of political parties, Maurice Duverger distinguished between cadre and mass parties (Duverger, 1964: 63–71). The difference was structural with cadre parties being a 'grouping of notabilities for the preparation of elections conducting campaigns and maintaining contact with the candidates' (Ibid.: 63, 64) while the mass party recruits as many members as possible. In sum, 'What the mass party secures by numbers, the cadre party achieves by selection' (Ibid.: 64). Both types were evident at the SNP's foundation. As Brand explained:

> There is an interesting comparison in structure between, on the one hand, the SNP and its predecessor, the National Party of Scotland, and the Scottish Party on the other. The last named was an excellent example of a caucus party. It had no mass membership and made no attempt to recruit one. Instead it depended on the leadership of a small group of well-known people; they *were* the Scottish Party with the addition of a few supporters, mostly from the same class and background of public life. (Brand, 1978: 267)

Amongst the Scottish Party's membership were a number of prominent figures including the Duke of Montrose and Sir Alexander McEwan, Provost of Inverness. There was a tension between those who favoured appealing to the elites and those who sought to build public support. The emphasis until the early 1940s was on recruiting and appealing to the elites. Thereafter, small pockets of members drawn together through personal contacts and friendships meant that the SNP had the form though not the substance of a mass party (Crawford, 1982: 66).

Parties evolve and old types give way to new forms (Katz and Mair, 1995; Koole, 1996; Krouwel, 2006). The structure of the SNP developed piecemeal over time and was affected by two related factors: fluctuation in its electoral support; and the ebb and flow of members. Its growth in the 1960s was evident in the number of its branches and this had implications for its organization and power structure. No authoritative account exists of the number of SNP members before 2004 but the party kept a reasonable tally of its branches. Branches were seen as organic, conforming to the size and shape of local communities which usually, but not always, corresponded with electoral divisions. Though it attempted to organize branches in workplaces, largely to compete with Labour, its branch structure had a predominantly geographic basis. Ian MacDonald, the National Organizer who oversaw the expansion of the SNP in the 1960s, encouraged branches to split once more than one viable unit was possible in an area as this was thought to encourage greater participation (Brand, 1978: 271). According to Brand, these branches may have been a 'hangover from the "movement" phase of the SNP' but were 'extremely popular with the activists', offering an 'intimacy which makes it possible to bring in neighbours and to know what is going on in the immediate area' (Ibid.).

A small core of senior members emerged during this period who became the effective leadership of the party. It remained a grass-roots party in which activists had considerable control over its direction, especially through its annual conference and national councils, the latter meeting between conferences, and with a loose collective leadership. Conferences consisted of branch delegates, dependent on the size of branches, and constituency association delegates plus other organizations with delegate rights such as the party's youth and student wings. After devolution, the SNP's transition from amateur-activist to professional-electoral party resembles the path taken by some Green parties (Lucardie and Rihoux, 2008). This transition was not entirely smooth. For the SNP, grass-roots democracy was 'both an ideological tenet and an organizational project', as it has been for Green parties (Ibid.: 3). While the SNP manifested some of the facets of 'New Politics' as described by Poguntke (1993: 10) – an emphasis on rights to participation and unilateral disarmament, and a general left-wing orientation – and had engaged in unconventional political activities in the form of civil disobedience and supported a modest measure of ecology, its preference was to operate through conventional electoral politics and, unlike the Greens, its members were not noted for having 'alternative life-styles'. The remnants of the movement phase that had served the SNP well when it developed as an extra-Parliamentary party were diluted as it inclined towards the electoral-professional model as the prospect of government increased. As Panebianco noted, the 'professionalization of party organizations' has been of the 'utmost importance' with professionals playing a greater role 'as the party's gravitational center shifts from the members to the electorate' (Panebianco, 1988: 264). But, as Panebianco makes clear, this model is an ideal type and no party fits the mass party or electoral professional type completely (Ibid.: 265).

In this chapter, we consider the SNP's transition to electoral-professional party. The changed opportunity structure that came with devolution was an important part of the backdrop to this change. But two other factors were important: a change in leader; and disappointing election results in the 2003 Scottish Parliament elections. Together, these three led to significant changes in the way the party was organized. There were a number of motives for the changes and assumptions made about the consequences of the changes. Interviews with senior party members suggest that some senior members, especially those with experience of managing party affairs, were motivated by a desire for greater professionalism and administrative efficacy. But many also saw organizational changes as necessary to ensure greater cohesion and discipline within the Parliamentary party at Holyrood.

The changing role of the SNP annual conference, the formal strengthening of the position of the leadership vis-à-vis activists, and the increased role given to ordinary, inactive members in choosing the leadership and selecting candidates will be considered. Peters has distinguished between 'formal' and 'informal' institutions (Peters, 1999: 18). This chapter considers not only what the SNP's formal, written constitution says about its structure and power but also the 'routines, procedures, conventions, roles, strategies, organisational forms, and technologies around which political activity is constructed...the beliefs, paradigms, codes, cultures, and knowledge that surround, support, elaborate, and contradict those roles and routines' (March and Olsen, 1989: 22). Responses from the membership survey and from elite interviews help us fill out our understanding of the formal arrangements.

Devolution's impact on the SNP as an organization

As we have seen, the SNP was largely a voluntary body before devolution. It had few MPs and few full-time staff compared with other parties in Scotland with a presence in Parliament. Until 1979, its National Conveners were neither MPs nor full-time politicians. From 1979 to 1999, its Conveners were MPs who had to spend a considerable part of the week for much of the year in London. Formally, the SNP did not have a leader until 2004 but instead had a collective leadership with a Chairman, later Convener. Devolution altered the SNP fundamentally. It secured its position as a Parliamentary party. Its leading figures were now elected members of the Scottish Parliament and it had become a serious contender for governmental power. The changed opportunity structure that devolution offered helped the SNP but it also presented challenges. The difficult relationship between the SNP National Executive Committee (NEC) and its Parliamentary group at Westminster during the 1974–79 Parliament had taught the party that tensions could develop when a new body of public figures emerged within a party run by activists but there were three key differences with the 1970s. First, Members of the Scottish Parliament (MSPs) were based in Scotland and more capable of maintaining direct contact with the party than its MPs had been. Second, the electoral system ensured that SNP representatives were returned from throughout Scotland with no area feeling that it was unrepresented by its MSPs. Third, almost the entire party leadership became MSPs in 1999. In the 1970s, its MPs were not, for the most part, people who had served in senior office in the party thus creating a 'bicephalous leadership' (Levy, 1990: 14).

With few seats in the Commons and only a handful of others within their grasp, the Parliamentary career prospects of SNP members were limited before devolution. Instead, members would fight it out for senior office in the party at each annual conference. Election as an MSP became the new, more attractive path for an ambitious SNP member. Power and personnel shifted from the party's institutions to Parliament. In interviews conducted with senior members of the party, this was almost unanimously acknowledged. There had been no changes in the party's constitution but the external political environment provided new opportunities. Power inside the SNP shifted away from the NEC and its internal institutions. This did not mean that a new core of key figures had emerged competing with the existing leadership, as in the late 1970s, but only that the same core people who had led the party prior to devolution were now MSPs and Parliamentary spokespersons. One MSP remarked that prior to devolution she would sit at conference with 'pen and paper and note down votes people had received for NEC' but 'nobody bothers with NEC elections now'. While those interviewed maintained that this process had hollowed out power within the party's structures, the general view was that the party's annual conference still retained an important, if unclear, position in decision-making.

Swinney's reforms

Mike Russell, SNP chief executive from 1994 to 1999, argued for an overhaul of the SNP's internal structure at a fringe meeting at the SNP's first conference after devolution. He noted that the party had gone through an 'almost unnoticed revolution' in the previous six months. From operating as an 'essentially extra-Parliamentary party' with only six MPs, it had become Scotland's main opposition but it had failed to take these changes into account in its own structures. Russell argued that party spokespersons, now predominantly MSPs, needed to be given more autonomy in making policy and that its conference should have 'overall supervision' but 'not line by line scrutiny'. He suggested a reduction in the number of national office-bearers and that one-member-one-vote (OMOV) elections should be used for electing all party offices including candidate selections. His plan to 'modernize' the SNP (*Scotland on Sunday*, 19 September 1999) provoked outrage amongst many in the party. He was described as 'MacMandelson' by critics within the party (*Evening News*, 23 September 1999), a reference to Peter Mandelson, Labour's key strategist who had overseen major changes in that party. His proposals failed to win the support of party leader Alex Salmond. Russell lost his seat on the SNP NEC, possibly as a consequence of his support for modernization, but continued to support OMOV though he accepted that his view did not have much support (*Herald*, 16 November 2001).

However, Russell's ideas took shape in reforms introduced by John Swinney in 2004. Swinney was elected SNP leader after Alex Salmond stood down in 2000. He was elected in a contest against Alex Neil, fellow MSP, by 547 (69 per cent) votes to 248 (31 per cent) among delegates at the SNP conference. Disillusionment set in when devolution did not lead rapidly to independence and this focused on the new leader. The SNP lost support in the 2001 UK general election and the 2003 Scottish Parliament elections. While it had tightened up its procedures for selecting those eligible to stand in 1999, a few colourful characters got through who went on to create difficulties for the leadership. While fundamentalism in the shape of opposition to devolution was now anachronistic, fundamentalists still existed. As one leading SNP figure put it, 'Fundamentalists had become rebels without a cause.' Internal fighting and recriminations spilled over into the (re-)selection process prior to the 2003 elections. Considerable time and effort was expended by SNP activists in battles over ranking candidates, depriving the SNP of efforts which would otherwise have been spent campaigning amongst the wider electorate. Accusations were made that new branches were established only to gain delegates for the election of list candidates. A number of List MSPs were effectively deselected by falling in the rankings to positions that made their return highly unlikely. Margo MacDonald, one of the best known SNP figures and a strong critic of Swinney, had topped the SNP List in Lothian Region in 1999 but fell to fifth place with no prospect of being returned in 2003. MacDonald resigned from the SNP and stood successfully as an Independent. The main losers, however, were Swinney supporters. Mike Russell, who had been the SNP's Education Spokesperson, was amongst eight SNP MSPs who lost their seats in 2003. Russell and Andrew Wilson, the SNP's Finance Spokesperson, had been placed too low to have much prospect of being returned. It was suggested that 'possibly the least known Nationalist MSP' had come top in one region 'after some assiduous working of the system' (*Herald*, 19 June 2002). Being known to the activists was more important than having a high public profile.

Immediately after the 2003 elections, Swinney announced a 'root and branch rejuvenation of the party as we face up to the challenges of the modern political era'. He maintained that this involved a 'painful transition' from being a 'party of protest to being a party of government'. Swinney argued that the SNP was 'caught in that transition'. It was 'no longer a party of protest but we're not yet viewed as a party of government' (*Scotsman, Daily Record*, 3 May 2003). That year, Swinney became the first leader since the 1960s to face a challenge. Bill Wilson, a little known activist, stood on a platform opposing Swinney's internal reforms. Wilson warned against the 'New Labourization' of the SNP, arguing that the SNP was most effective when pressurizing Labour into making concessions rather than seeking to win power. He accused the party's MSPs of treating the membership like 'donkeys that have to do as they're told' (*Herald*, 27 July 2003). Swinney defeated Wilson comfortably by 577 (84 per cent) to 111 (16 per cent) votes. The contest briefly allowed Swinney to re-assert his authority. It also highlighted the provision allowing maverick candidates to contest the leadership and the possibility that an incumbent SNP First Minister might be forced into a contest by a very small group of members.

In his speech at the 2003 conference, Swinney focused more on internal matters than he had in his previous speeches as leader, arguing for a 'reliable national database of members', rejecting claims that this would centralize power. He proposed that a special conference should decide whether to introduce OMOV and other reforms (Swinney, 2003). Swinney's victory over Bill Wilson in 2003 did not stop criticism. On the eve of the special conference, Campbell Martin, an MSP returned after coming to the top of the list in his region in 2003, threatened to leave the party if Swinney did not resign and Alex Salmond return as leader. More damaging was Mike Russell's suggestion that Swinney would receive a visit from 'men in grey kilts' if the SNP lost one of its two Members of the European Parliament (MEPs) at elections in June (Russell, 2004). A special conference in Spring 2004 gave overwhelming support to Swinney's proposals. It agreed to:

- streamline the NEC and have fewer senior office-bearers;
- introduce OMOV for the election of leader and deputy leader, and in selecting candidates;
- create the position of party 'Leader', replacing the National Convener;
- give the Leader power to appoint a Business Convener, who would be in charge of operational matters, from amongst members of the NEC (see Figure 3.1).

A more vaguely worded commitment to strive towards a 'balanced list of candidates, particularly in regard to gender' was passed by a narrower majority of 146 to 127. The party's continued commitment to radical constitutional change was affirmed when it replaced 'self-government' with 'independence' in its aims. Though the SNP had not previously

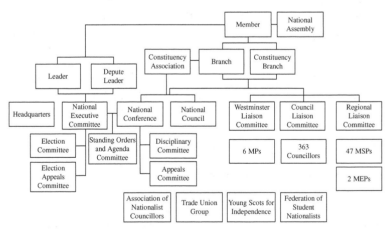

Figure 3.1. SNP organization structure, 2007

Source: SNP headquarters.

included the word 'independence' in its constitution, few doubted that this was its objective. This amendment was designed more to emphasize that SNP modernization differed from that of its Labour counterpart in being about organizational matters rather than the abandonment of any principles. As one figure involved in the process conceded, it was a 'sop' to hardliners to emphasize that the party was not abandoning its core objective. The changes amounted to the most radical overhaul in the SNP's constitution since 1948 and reflected Swinney's desire to make the transition from protest movement to government.

The SNP vote fell by 7.5 per cent at the European elections in June 2004. Swinney announced his resignation within a fortnight. In addition to the reforms to its constitution under his leadership, the SNP had reformed its headquarters and campaign techniques, and established a national call centre in Glasgow in 2002. Interviews with senior party members show that even Swinney's critics accept that his legacy was a more professional organization that contributed to the 2007 election victory. The implementation of the national membership list and abandonment of a fixed subscription from the start of 2004, though a minimum amount has been set, reduced leakage of membership and increased income derived from members by 329 per cent in one year alone (SNP, 2004b). While part of the reason lay in an increase in SNP members generated by the leadership contest following Swinney's resignation, the new system allowed its headquarters to identify those members likely to contribute most generously to financial appeals. Significantly, while the SNP's membership grew considerably after the introduction of the central membership list, as did the income generated from its members, the number of branches remained broadly the same (Table 3.1). As this money is paid directly to headquarters and flows in evenly across the year, the party has also been able to manage its finances better than in the past though donations increase dramatically as an election approaches.

Party finances were also transformed in another way after devolution though this was a consequence of the party's improved electoral prospects rather than improved organization. In the lead up to the 2007 elections, the SNP received a number of substantial donations allowing it to outspend other parties for the first time (Table 3.2). A group of wealthy businessmen contributed significant sums of money to the SNP's 2007 election campaign allowing it to professionalize its campaign efforts.

Table 3.1. Growth in membership and income

	2003	2004	2005	2006	2007	2008	2009
Members	9,450	10,854	10,995	12,571	13,944	15,097	15,644
No. of branches	225	246	228	226	230	222	218
New members in year	–	–	–	2,875	2,206	2,203	2,205
New members joining online (%)	–	–	–	46.3	46.7	65.5	64.5
Members paying by direct debit (%)	6.5	33.5	35.5	40.3	57.3	59.5	61.1
Average payment by direct debit	£17	£30	£32	£36	£47	£56	£54
Average payment not by direct debit	–	–	–	–	£10	£9	£9
Members paying £5 unwaged rate (%)	–	31.2	28.9	24.5	19.0	21.7	21.5
Members paying via local branch (%)	82.7	8.1	3.5	3.3	2.5	1.2	1.1

Source: SNP (2009: 4–5) and SNP HQ.

Table 3.2. Party expenditure in 2003 and 2007 Scottish elections

	2003 (£)	2007 (£)	Percentage increase on 2003
SNP	473,107	1,383,462	192.4
Labour	726,702	1,102,866	51.8
Conservatives	323,279	601,983	86.2
Liberal Democrats	130,360	303,740	133.0

Source: Electoral Commission.

Candidate selection

The academic literature on candidate selection explains why this is important and also the criteria used in assessing processes of candidate selection comparatively. Schattschneider remarked that the nominating process is 'obviously one of the points at which parties can be studied most advantageously'. It should allow us to 'discover the locus of power within the party, for he who has the power to make the nomination owns the party' (Schattschneider, 1960 [1942]: 101). Bowler has argued that the nomination process is the main determinant of the behaviour of legislators (Bowler, 2000). However, candidate selection has also been described as the 'secret garden of politics' (Gallagher and Marsh, 1988), that it is not always easy to identify the 'precise place in the party where the key decisions are made' (Gallagher, 1988: 275). Rahat and Hazan identify four criteria for assessing procedures for candidate selection: the selectorate; candidacy; decentralization; and voting versus appointment (Rahat and Hazan, 2001). The selectorate consists of those who select the candidates and can be viewed along a continuum from the most inclusive in which all citizens are involved to the most exclusive involving a 'selectorate of a single individual' (Hazan and Rahat, 2006: 111).

Candidate selection had been a staged process in the SNP. In a well-established practice, self-selected members put themselves forward as potential candidates on the party's approved list. This stage gave the leadership an important gatekeeping role. However, the opinion amongst interviewees involved in the process was that a fairly liberal approach was adopted. Indeed a number of interviewees later suggested the party had been lax in allowing a number of individuals onto the list who should have been blocked. These comments referred to a small group of SNP MSPs who in the first Parliament, elected in 1999, proved predictably troublesome for the leadership. The SNP had been influenced by the process in which the Labour leadership prevented a number of high-profile members from standing. Labour suffered much adverse publicity, especially when Dennis Canavan, one of its MPs, was blocked from standing for the Scottish Parliament but stood successfully as an Independent. The SNP was keen to avoid being tarnished in the same way. However, while Labour suffered adverse publicity in the run-up to the 1999 elections, the SNP suffered more sustained bad publicity as a consequence of the election of a small group of maverick MSPs during the 1999–2003 election. Labour MSPs, on the other hand, proved remarkably well disciplined.

Residential weekends were organized in 1998 at which potential candidates were interviewed by a panel of six senior members, reflecting a balance of pragmatists and fundamentalists, which resulted in a list of 178 candidates of whom 49 were women. A number of applicants rejected prior to 1999 were successful on a second attempt prior to 2003 including one who became an MSP and Minister in 2007. The main reasons for rejection were inexperience and poor performance at the weekend selection process. Members were eligible to put themselves forward if they had been a member for ten months, had two references from party members and were nominated by one branch. At a special conference in 1998, the party debated whether it should adopt a 'zipping' system for the regional list whereby female and male candidates would alternate in the rankings ensuring that an even number of men and women were returned. This was rejected by 282 votes to 257 despite the support of the leadership. At this time, OMOV was also rejected for selecting candidates (*Herald*, 7 June 1998). This was a victory for the activists. In the event, 43 per cent of SNP MSPs elected in 1999 were women but this was achieved with considerable effort through informal arrangements, encouraging women to stand, rather than any formal institutional arrangements.

The SNP's selectorate for constituency contests in 1999 consisted of branch delegates or, where only one branch existed in a constituency, activists in that branch. For regional contests, delegates from branches met in selection contests of about 100–150 members and candidates were chosen using single transferable vote. A survey of candidates in 1999 found that there was more approval of the selection process for constituencies than regional lists: only 4 per cent of respondent thought the process for constituencies was not democratic and 6 per cent thought it unfair compared with 12 per cent who thought the list selection process was undemocratic and 24 per cent who thought it unfair (Bradbury et al., 2000: 59). This may have reflected the relative importance of the List: the SNP won twenty-eight List and only seven constituency seats in 1999.

In common with the contemporary Scottish and British political mood, the SNP sought to find 'new' candidates from beyond the usual suspects while simultaneously imposing stricter criteria on who would be allowed to stand. In the event, SNP candidates were drawn predominantly from the party's core of long-standing activists. Indeed, the mean number of years SNP candidates had been members of the party was longer than for any of the other three main Scottish parties and about half had served as a constituency office-bearer (compared with a quarter of Conservative candidates, one-fifth of Labour candidates, and 35 per cent of Liberal Democrats) (Bennie et al., 2001: 31).

As we have seen, the SNP's experience of candidate selection in 2003 proved damaging. The changes under John Swinney involved more central control of who was permitted to stand but widening the selectorate to the entire membership. The view that widening the selectorate strengthens the leadership as this weakens activists capable of mounting a challenge to the leadership (Katz, 2001; Carty, 2004) has some traction in the case of the SNP. However, a number of hardliners critical of Swinney's leadership were returned in 2007, including Swinney's 2003 challenger Bill Wilson. This did not conform entirely with the thesis that an inclusive selectorate increased the power of party elites and preserved party cohesion (Hazan and Rahat, 2006: 117). The absence of splits and degree of discipline amongst SNP MSPs since 2007 may testify less to the selection process producing compliant MSPs than to the unity brought about by electoral success. It also suggests that the difference between active and inactive members may be contextually contingent with activists more likely to assert themselves in relations with the leadership when the party performs poorly. In essence, electoral success is a more important resource for the leadership in its relations with the members than any constitutional provision. In addition, as Norris has noted, the distinction between candidates/elected representatives and constituency workers 'seems far fuzzier and mixed' in practice than often suggested (Norris, 1995: 42).

Electing an SNP leader

The resignation of John Swinney in June 2004 shortly after the SNP had adopted a new constitution, meant that the new leader would be elected for the first time by OMOV. As Roseanna Cunningham, Swinney's deputy, announced that she was standing for the leadership, OMOV would also be used in the election of a new deputy leader. Mike Russell decided to stand, though he was not an MSP at this stage, as did Nicola Sturgeon, List MSP for Glasgow. Alex Salmond, who had been National Convener from 1990 to 2000, initially ruled himself out but decided to stand after considerable pressure from members. He was no longer an MSP but had remained an MP. This meant that if elected leader and seeking to become First Minister he would need to find a seat in the Scottish Parliament. Sturgeon pulled out of the leadership contest in favour of Salmond and stood instead for the deputy's post with Salmond's support. Two other MSPs – Fergus Ewing and Christine Grahame – stood for the deputy leadership. Grahame was the only candidate who could be described as a hardliner. She said that she would 'not defer' to Salmond if she was elected deputy leader and he was elected leader (*Scotsman*, 13 August 2004), suggesting serious disunity had she been elected.

Each candidate required the nomination of at least a hundred members drawn from at least twenty branches (SNP, 2004c: 1.1.2). This was designed to ensure a broader base of support than was previously required. The party announced that it had 8,209 members at the point when postal ballot papers were sent to members. The count was conducted by the Electoral Reform Society. Just under 80 per cent of members voted with Alex Salmond winning convincingly on first preferences (Table 3.3). Salmond's authority was greater than when he was first elected leader in 1990: OMOV gave him greater legitimacy; he already had a successful track record as leader; the party's new rules made it

Table 3.3. Result of the 2004 SNP leadership elections

Leader	First preference N	votes %	Deputy leader	First preference N	votes %
Alex Salmond	4,952	75.8	Nicola Sturgeon	3,521	53.9
Roseanna Cunningham	953	14.6	Fergus Ewing	1,605	24.6
Michael Russell	631	9.6	Christine Grahame	1,410	21.6
Total votes cast	6,536			6,536	

more difficult to be challenged; and there was no significant internal opponent. The SNP's support in the opinion polls increased, caused by what the media called the 'Salmond bounce.'

Salmond's vote narrowly exceeded the proportion that had voted for him under the old delegate system fourteen years before (72.3 per cent of conference delegates had voted for Salmond against Margaret Ewing). It is impossible to determine whether Sturgeon would have defeated Cunningham and Russell had Salmond not intervened though it can be assumed that she would not have won as much support as Salmond. She became leader of the SNP in Holyrood while Salmond became a Nationalist leader in exile until he was elected to Holyrood in 2007. According to interviews with senior members, Sturgeon's standing was enhanced considerably during this period and she became the clear favourite to succeed Salmond.

Leadership

The SNP had historically had a collective leadership, with the exception of the party's very early years when John MacCormick was intolerant of opposition (Brand, 1978: 277). Gordon Wilson, SNP National Chairman 1979–90, has explained how he and Billy Wolfe, his predecessor, supported collective leadership of the SNP, 'The SNP constitution did not have provision for a single, pre-eminent leader' (Wilson, 2009: 154). Wilson defined the role of party chairman:

> The Chairman was guardian of the Party Constitution and in the Executive Committee was first amongst equals. And while this role gave the Chairman considerable initiative and influence, he had to work with the other office-bearers who were elected to executive office in their own right. It was not an infrequent occurrence for the Chairman, any Chairman, to be out-voted. The role of Party Leader did not exist in the SNP nor was there any requirement that the Chairman be an MP. (Ibid.: 155)

Wilson's interpretation of the SNP constitution was shared across the party. The collective leadership meant that charismatic and media-friendly figures could eclipse those with more senior formal party positions. Respondents to a poll asking who the 'main leaders of the SNP' were in 1981 found that Margo MacDonald and Winnie Ewing, neither of whom had chaired the party and the former had been defeated as deputy two years before, were identified by more people than party chairman Gordon Wilson (*Scotsman*, 11 March 1981).

Nonetheless, Crawford maintains that there was 'clear evidence of core persistence' with five key figures consistently on the NEC and senior office-bearers in the 1960s and that a further group of five dominant figures emerged around 1970 (Crawford, 1982: 244–5). According to Crawford, the myth of a decentralized structure emerged because workload was shared by a number of figures and levels while power was concentrated in the hands of its core. However, this understates activists' power through control of conference to determine the party's strategy, image, and policies.

From the 1980s, key figures in the leadership used their party positions as bully pulpits to make the case for a more pragmatic strategy. Being elected on a pragmatic platform to a position in the party, including the party convenership, was insufficient. Formally, the National Convener did not have the autonomy found in other parties to devise party strategy but had to share responsibility with other senior party members in Parliament and national party office-bearers, and was accountable to the party conference and quarterly national councils. The leadership was neither unified nor unconstrained. National office-bearers were elected by national conference and usually consisted of politicians with diverse views on strategy and much else.

On becoming Convener in 1990, Alex Salmond's approach differed from that of his predecessors. He adopted a high-profile approach and saw his role as leading the party, rather than convening the party in the way described by Wilson. While the SNP moved towards a pragmatic position on devolution under Salmond, this was achieved through persuasion, and often against strong opposition, rather than any formal shift in institutional power. Indeed, Salmond has shown little interest in his party's internal constitution. Though constrained by the party's formal constitution and its decentralized participatory ethos, Salmond came to be seen as leader in much the same way as leaders of other Parliamentary parties in Britain.

On his return to the leadership in 2004, however, he had both formal institutional protection, through the constitutional reforms instituted by his predecessor, and his own personal authority. This authority was enhanced when he became First Minister in 2007. There is little doubt that Salmond commands overwhelming support in the SNP. None of those interviewed for this study doubted his unambiguous position as leader. Interviewees described Salmond 'dominating his party and Scottish politics', and suggesting that he 'blocks out the sun' in the internal politics of the SNP. The SNP membership survey was conducted within months of the SNP winning the 2007 election and the membership was predictably enthusiastic about its leaders. When asked to score senior members on a 0–10 scale in which '0' represented strongly disliked and '10' strongly liked, the party's key figures were very popular with the membership, and even more so among those who regularly attended branch meetings (Table 3.4). Members of the Scottish Cabinet came ahead of other key figures in the party with the exception of veteran Nationalist Winnie Ewing. Salmond's ratings by SNP members exceed even those of Tony Blair by Labour members after Labour's 1997 victory.

When the party's elite were asked to rank the five most powerful figures in the SNP during interviews, a different pattern emerged (Table 3.5). Salmond was seen by all interviewees as the most powerful figure in the SNP. Sturgeon was the only other figure mentioned by all interviewees, apart from herself, as amongst the five most powerful figures. Weightings were attached to the rankings: first ranked was awarded 5; second most powerful 4; and so on. Sturgeon's position as deputy leader is more than nominal, as it can be in other parties. Three key figures, all Cabinet Ministers, emerge: Salmond; Sturgeon; and Swinney. While another group of leading figures are identified, these were deemed significantly less powerful than the top three. Peter Murrell, SNP chief executive, comes some way behind the top three

Table 3.4. Mean rating of politicians by SNP members

	Never attend	Attend meetings monthly
A. Salmond (c)	9.3	9.4
N. Sturgeon (c)	8.7	8.9
W. Ewing	8.4	8.7
J. Swinney (c)	8.3	8.9
K. Macaskill (c)	7.8	8.2
F. Hyslop (c)	7.7	8.1
A. Robertson	7.7	8.2
A. MacNeil	7.7	8.0
R. Lochhead (c)	7.7	8.0
R. Cunningham	7.6	7.3
M. Russell	7.4	7.9
A. Neil	7.3	7.9

(c) = member of Cabinet at time of survey.

Table 3.5. Rankings of SNP leaders as 'powerful within the party' by party elites
(*N* = 73)

	Weighted score	Frequency of mentions
Alex Salmond	365	73
Nicola Sturgeon	271	72
John Swinney	183	54
Peter Murrell	60	289
Angus Robertson	41	22
Kevin Pringle	40	18
Kenny MacAskill	36	20
Bruce Crawford	29	14
Michael Russell	21	12

and Kevin Pringle, senior Special Adviser to the First Minster, appears ahead of any of the three remaining Cabinet Ministers. It is unlikely that the membership as a whole would be aware of either Murrell or Pringle as neither has a significant media profile. Angus Robertson and Bruce Crawford have both been Business Conveners of the SNP, a position appointed by the party leader, with the former becoming leader of the SNP MPs after Salmond became First Minister. As Minister for Parliamentary Business, Crawford is widely credited, especially by SNP MSPs, for ensuring the SNP minority government has been able to get much of its programme through Parliament. Notably, other than Salmond and Sturgeon, Mike Russell is the only figure who stood for the leadership or deputy leadership in 2004 and came in the top ten SNP politicians.

National conference and national councils: changing functions

A number of changes had occurred affecting the party's annual conference following devolution. Formally, conference had become less important with the removal of its power to elect the party leader and deputy leader. The streamlined NEC and shift in focus to MSPs meant that conferences had lost some attraction to activists but the extent of change can be exaggerated. Despite the ease with which members could challenge an incumbent, there had been few leadership elections in the SNP's history and only four leadership elections in the thirty-five years prior to the 2004 contest. As we have seen, a familiar list of senior members held senior office over many years. Nonetheless, even if attending conference involved returning only the same grouping of leaders each year, these contests attracted large turnouts of delegates.

In time, fewer senior figures from the pre-devolution period sought election to national party office focusing instead on election as Parliamentarians. MSPs now attended national councils less often and many senior members admitted that they would now have difficulty listing members of the NEC whereas in the past they would know all members. With fewer resolutions being submitted to annual conference for debate, and less interest in contests for national office, national conference had become more like a 'rally', a term used unprompted by many interviewees, than a policymaking forum. However, not all of those interviewed agreed with this view. As one MSP expressed it, 'if it appears like a rally, it's because people are pretty content at the moment. It doesn't mean conference has become a rally.' Very few agreed with one MSP who dismissed conference as 'almost irrelevant' but none doubted that conference had lost much of its power. One MSP observed that delegates had previously seen the conference as 'the Scottish Parliament Continuing' but since devolution they 'can make no such grand claims now'.

Another function noted by a former senior office-bearer was that conference was a 'good testing ground' for ideas. Nonetheless, the same interviewee noted that key policymakers now included the government's special advisers many of whom had rarely spoken at conference prior to becoming advisers and were unable to do so as advisers. Being in government had a powerful effect with one interviewee referring to the need for 'self-policing' given the hostile media environment. As a councillor remarked, 'We are still adjusting to having Ministers. Before, you could say anything at conference and it didn't matter. That's not the case any more. We are all mindful that the SNP is in government.' A crucial test was whether SNP MSPs would ever ignore policy passed by the conference and interviewees were less certain of circumstances when this might occur. It was widely acknowledged that this could happen and that the conference had the potential to embarrass an SNP Government but, once more, general contentment meant that this had not yet occurred. It was noted by many of those interviewed that the Standing Orders and Agenda Committee of the party has tended to allow at least one controversial item each year to be debated at conference. Such items have had the potential to embarrass the government. An example of this occurred in 2008 when a resolution critical of the SNP Government's policy on alcohol sales to people under 21 was submitted by the party's youth wing. A number of senior figures were lined up to defend the government policy and potential embarrassment was averted (*Herald*, 18 October 2008). Many interviewees felt conference still played a useful role as a place for 'networking'. It has a further important function. The party generated considerable income – around 10 per cent of its annual income – from its national conference. This became even more important after devolution. The number and range of fringe events increased considerably, as did the income generated, and particularly after the SNP formed a government.

The existence of MSPs and Ministers altered the nature of conference in other ways. Time is allotted to Ministerial addresses in addition to speeches from the leader, deputy leader, and other office-bearers, reducing time available for contributions from delegates. It was felt by some interviewees, especially a number of women, that it was far more intimidating speaking at an SNP conference than in the past partly because of greater media scrutiny and the presence of Ministers. As one senior figure remarked, 'it's the same people but they now have a status that they didn't previously'. A figure who had attended conferences over many years remarked that conference had been a 'gathering of friends as well as a policy making body, it was still small enough to be quite intimate' but some of that intimacy had gone.

The survey of members found that most members felt that those who attended party meetings and conferences should have more say in the party than those who are never active. Only 7.9 per cent of members disagreed with this proposition. This view has to be set against the strong view, at least amongst those who had a view, that national conference and national council had the right amount of power. Indeed, party members were remarkably content with the internal structure of the party. When asked whether individual party posts, headquarters staff, and various party organs had too much, too little, or about the right amount of power, the membership as a whole was consistently very satisfied. Notably, the membership seemed most pleased with the power allocated to the leader, deputy leader, and MSPs. The more active members were a little less content with the leadership and internal party structures, and more likely to support enhanced rights for local branches and ordinary members.

These membership views, of course, may simply reflect general satisfaction following a historic election victory and also the fact that few members would have much experience of the workings of the party. This became clear in elite interviews. While the membership and activists were broadly content, there was much more concern amongst the elite who were interviewed that the party's institutions still required attention. A number expressed concern that the party still had not worked out a clear role for conference as a policymaking body. These concerns came as much from those loyal to the leadership as from previous critics. Many were wrestling with how to include amateur-activism in an electoral-professional party. One loyal figure noted the tension between 'democratic sovereignty in the party versus media event'. Repeatedly, those interviewed expressed concern that the SNP conference might turn completely into a rally. Very few of those interviewed took the view that there was any effort to suppress debate at conference on the part of the leadership. Some observed that it had become a 'self-regulating' institution in which party members had, as one MSP claimed, become 'more responsible – maybe too responsible in that there are areas where we need to think things through rather than accept things'. But conference remained important as a showcase. It was important as 'people notice who makes good speeches and who has good ideas', remarked a former senior party office-holder. It remains a 'very public forum' and a 'good testing ground', and even though OMOV is used in the election of leader, those attending conference are important as they can influence many of the other party members. It was also suggested that conference allowed the 'rising stars of the party' to get noticed.

Conclusion

While there may be cohorts of pragmatists and fundamentalists amongst a party's activists, the pivotal body in any party is often the non-aligned party membership consisting of those who are motivated by an 'active concern with only the gross differences between electoral parties, from a passive attitude towards policy issues, or from a calculated desire to avoid identification with particular tendencies or actions in order to gain popularity within the whole electorate' (Rose, 1964: 38). This element has been pivotal inside the SNP (Mitchell, 1990). It has been this element that has been given power at the expense of the activists as a consequence of the party's constitutional changes under John Swinney's leadership. Devolution offered the SNP previously unavailable opportunities to govern and therefore a new relevance (Mitchell, 2009b). However, the transition was not painless. Devolution may have changed the opportunity structure but this in itself was not enough to bring the SNP to power. The legacy of its constitution, suited to days when it was either a pre- or precarious Parliamentary party, limited its ability to take advantage of the new opportunities offered by devolution. Some senior party figures who advocated change wanted a more professional organization but others also saw reform as a means of shifting power within the party away from activists towards Parliamentarians and ensuring that a more cohesive group of Parliamentarians was returned. While other factors were important in determining the SNP's success in 2007, its transformation from what was essentially an amateur-activist model to an electoral-professional model played a significant part.

4

Who are the SNP Members?

Introduction

As we saw in previous chapters, the Scottish National Party (SNP) has seen the size of its membership fluctuate significantly over the period since it first gained a seat in the House of Commons. Evidence from the 1960s and 1970s, and some well-entrenched myths about the party have informed understanding of the SNP's membership. The aim of this chapter is to use our data from the membership survey to create a demographic profile of the SNP. While avoiding stereotyping, we can say that a picture emerges of the 'typical' SNP member. This does not mean that all SNP members are of this type but that the profile we create helps us to get a sense of the type of people involved.

The analysis is divided into three sections. In the first, we look at basic socio-demographic characteristics, notably age and sex but also ethnicity and religion. The focus in the second section turns to major socio-economic variables: education; occupation; class; and income. The third is concerned with geography, past, and present, considering both where members (and their parents) were born and how they are now distributed across Scotland.

Very little was known about the SNP's membership before this study. The party itself had no reliable data on its members until it introduced its central membership list in 2004. Its understanding of its membership was based on fragmentary and incomplete data submitted by branches. Even after 2004, the data that the party held on its members have been limited. For example, one senior party official informed us that over a decade ago the party estimated that 48 per cent of its members were women, but that figure far exceeds the proportion of women discovered in this study. It is possible that the party's profile has changed significantly but a more likely explanation is that the party's data were incomplete.

Previously, inferences could be drawn about the SNP membership from three sources: observation of activists attending SNP national conferences and other meetings; survey data on SNP voters; and surveys of other parties' memberships. There are obvious limitations to each in understanding the SNP. Activists are unlikely to form a representative subset of the broader membership but they can at least give some indication of what is distinctive about the party's profile and may contribute to the projection of an image of the party to the electorate. However, as we saw in the previous chapter, empirical research often undermines impressionistic accounts of the SNP.

More reliable data on who votes for the SNP has existed since the mid-1970s and a clear picture can be built of where the SNP draws its support. Though no political party precisely resembles those who vote for it, we can expect some similarities. In the past, the SNP disproportionately attracted support from younger voters and those with weak social class and religious affiliations (Cornford and Brand, 1969; Miller, 1981; Bennie et al., 1997; Paterson, 2006). One early study found that the SNP attracted support from previous non-voters (Cornford and Brand, 1969). A survey in 1976 found that 46 per cent of voters between 18 and 34 intended to vote SNP with less than half that proportion of voters in the age groups 55–64 and over 65 intending to do so (Webb and Hall, 1978: 11). However, this age gap had more or less closed by the 1990s (Paterson, 2006) and in 2007 had reversed, following a particularly steep rise in support for the SNP amongst older voters between 2003 and 2007 (Johns et al., 2010: ch. 2).

As Butler and Stokes (1974: 57) noted, it was those with weaker senses of class or religious identity, and thus with weaker attachments to the two major parties who were more volatile in their voting behaviour and hence more open to new parties such as the SNP. The SNP was therefore able to advance electorally more easily amongst those who were not religious or only weakly aligned to any denomination (Miller, 1981: 146) and among those without a strong subjective class identification. Social class and religion were well-established cleavages in Scottish politics (Budge and Urwin, 1966; Bochel and Denver, 1970; Miller, 1981; Bennie et al., 1997). As has been frequently demonstrated, class was the most important cleavage in explaining voting behaviour during this period (Pulzer, 1968; Butler and Stokes, 1974). In addition, a religious cleavage in voting behaviour in twentieth-century Scotland had developed with Protestants more likely to vote Conservative and Catholics voting Labour.

Predictably, we also find that the SNP was better placed to attract support amongst those voters aligned to the periphery end of the emerging centre–periphery cleavage. This divide was made manifest in national identity. Those who saw themselves at the British end of the Scottish–British continuum of identities were unlikely to support the SNP. Given that the SNP existed to promote Scottish independence and Scottish interests, we would expect it to gain most support on one side of this cleavage. However, 'Scottish interests' cannot be defined objectively and were defined differently over time by the party. During the 1980s and 1990s, when the Conservatives were in government but had little support in Scotland, the SNP adopted a more explicitly left-wing profile as the defender of working-class interests. The centre–periphery cleavage appeared to reinforce the class cleavage (Brand and Mitchell, 1993). Lynch has asserted that the SNP has moved from social democracy to 'no ideology' in recent years (Lynch, 2009), though evidence presented in Chapter 8 suggests this is not quite correct.

Finally, clues about the SNP's members can also be found in the major membership surveys of other parties in Britain (e.g. Rüdig et al., 1991; Seyd and Whiteley, 1992, 2002; Whitelely et al., 1994, 2006; Bennie, 2004) and elsewhere (e.g. Widfeldt, 1995, 1999; Cross and Young, 2004). These studies routinely show that party members are disproportionately male, middle-aged (with the youngest age groups most underrepresented), middle class, and educated, though there are significant differences between the parties. In short, the socio-demographic profile of party members more closely resembles that of political elites than of ordinary citizens or even those who vote for the party. This applies whether the comparison is with the wider population as a whole or with that party's supporters. Moreover, there are few exceptions to these general rules which, according to the largest European comparative study (Widfeldt, 1995), apply across countries and party families. Research on the hard-left Scottish Socialist Party confirmed the middleclass nature of its members (Cornock, 2003). This also extends to Canadian parties, including, in the largest previous survey of sub-state nationalist parties' members, the Bloc Québecois (Cross and Young, 2004).

Drawing on evidence from earlier accounts of the SNP, voting behaviour and other party membership studies, we can identify some plausible hypotheses about the SNP's membership. Given its *raison d'être* and the profile of its core electoral support, we would expect its members to identify strongly as Scottish. While members who joined in the period when the Conservatives were in government after 1979 are more likely to see themselves as working class, the likelihood is that the SNP, in common with other parties, is basically a middle-class party. Whether it attracts high levels of support from particular occupations, either those associated with Poujadist-type parties outside the mainstream or rather more professional occupations, is unclear from other research. However, given the central importance of national identity and the nature of its electoral support, we would expect that its members would be disinclined to adopt strong class or religious identities. It is less clear whether the SNP would be expected to be as male-dominated as other parties as its electoral support would suggest or whether having had high-profile senior women members over a long period of time should have aided it in attracting women. Equally, it is unclear from other data whether this constitutionally radical party should appeal to young people given its past electoral appeal or would have the same problem attracting young people that afflicts other parties.

Demographic profile

As noted above, members of political parties are generally older than the electorate as a whole, and the ageing of party members is a European-wide phenomenon (Scarrow and Gezgor, 2010). The evidence suggests that this is a generational effect, signalling that those reaching voting age in recent decades have less interest in the participation offered by party membership (Dalton and Wattenberg, 2000; Bruter and Harrison, 2009a; Goerres, 2009: ch. 5). This suggests that a party with an ageing membership, unable to regenerate with new, younger members, is in danger of declining subscriptions and a narrowing pool of activists. As Table 4.1 suggests, this may be a concern to the SNP. Less than one in ten

Table 4.1. Age distribution of party memberships (%)

Age (year)	SNP (2007–08)	Conservative (1992)	Liberal Democrats (1998–99)	Labour (1997)		Scottish Green (2002)
				Overall	Scottish only	
18–25	3	1	2	4	5	4
26–35	6	4	5	13	11	18
36–45	12	11	11	21	22	28
46–55	16	17	23	24	21	25
56–65	27	24	22	16	17	13
66+	36	43	36	23	24	12
Mean age	59	62	59	52	51	47
N	6740	2424	2866	5594	362	258

As a result of rounding, percentages in this and all subsequent tables may not sum exactly to 100.

of its members are below the age of 35 (and these young members are considerably outnumbered by those over 75). Overall, nearly two-thirds of members are over 55, and well over one-third older than 65.

Another implication of the generational argument above is that the average age of a party's members is likely to increase gradually over time. This complicates comparisons of the kind reported in Table 4.1. As results for the other parties predate the SNP survey, often by quite a long time, there is reason to suppose that the relative age of Nationalist members is overstated. Nonetheless, it is clear that the SNP is not exempt from the 'greying' trend observed in party membership more generally and the average age of its members exceeded that of Labour members in 1997. The average age of Scottish Labour members in the 1997 survey of Labour members was 51. The results place the SNP among the traditional parties, rather than the Greens, a party whose members tend to be younger than those of conventional parties. However, even the Greens have experienced an ageing of membership: between 1990 and 2002 the proportion of Scottish Green members below the age of 45 declined from 75 to 45 per cent (Bennie, 2004: 189–90). The evidence suggests that neither new nor long-established parties have been able to counter the waning interest of young people in party membership.

The generational argument is intended to explain declining membership rolls, with ageing and eventually dying members not being replaced. However, the SNP has bucked the general trend and experienced a substantial increase in membership, especially since the mid-2000s. In conjunction with the results in Table 4.1, this suggests that the recent recruits to the party have come disproportionately from older age groups. The trend from electoral studies might be instructive here. Early surveys showed that the SNP surge in the 1970s owed much to support from younger people, and that the average SNP voter was much younger than the average for the electorate as a whole (Miller, 1981; Kendrick, 1983). However, as noted earlier in the chapter, this age gap had closed by the 1990s and, if anything, had reversed by the 2007 election. The reasons for this abrupt shift are unclear. What is clear is that the SNP is no longer a 'young people's party' either in terms of its membership or its base of electoral support as it appeared to have been in the 1970s. It would seem that there have been two developments. First, generational change means that the youthful Nationalists of the 1970s are now in more senior age categories. Second, the SNP has disproportionately recruited amongst older people in recent years.

One of the most striking features of the SNP's membership is how male it is (Table 4.2). The Conservatives are the only party in which

Table 4.2. Sex breakdown of party memberships (%)

	SNP (2007–08)	Conservative (1992)	Liberal Democrats (1998–99)	Labour (1997)		Scottish Green (2002)
				Overall	Scottish only	
Male	68	48	54	61	61	63
Female	32	52	46	39	39	37
N	6885	2405	2866	5757	371	258

women are in a majority but no other party comes close to the over 2:1 ratio by which males outnumber females in the SNP.

The same gender gap also appears in the SNP's electoral support, with the extent to which males predominate again being unusual compared with other parties in Britain and elsewhere (Miller, 1981: 147–8; Johns et al., 2010: 32). One possibility is that the party has changed over time and has become a male-dominated party having formerly had a much higher proportion of women but without comparable data from an earlier period it is difficult to reach any definitive conclusion. What we can consider is whether there is any evidence amongst the existing membership that the breakdown by sex varies depending on the period in which members joined the party (and were still members in 2007/08). In the years before the party's major breakthrough, more than seven out of ten joiners were male (Table 4.3). But that breakthrough, heralded by Winnie Ewing's by-election success, seems to have triggered a change (even if the SNP was still a predominantly male party). However, the proportion of women who joined after 2005 has fallen back to pre-1967 levels. The difficulty, as always in such analyses, is in judging whether this signals a greater willingness on the part of men or a greater reluctance on the part of women to join the party. There is a tendency in media coverage of gender and politics to treat women's behaviour as the phenomenon to be explained (Miller et al., 1991), even though evidence suggests that the increase in SNP electoral support in 2007

Table 4.3. Sex breakdown of SNP membership by date of joining (%)*

	1930–66	1967–79	1980–92	1993–2004	2005 onwards
Male	71	65	67	69	72
Female	29	35	33	31	28
N	789	1421	1123	1578	1627

*The breakdown is based on key junctures in SNP history.

compared with 2003 is explained by greater support amongst men (Johns et al., 2010). The central point is that the party membership is, and has long been, male-dominated.

Survey respondents were asked to nominate which of a long list of possible ethnicities best described themselves. Only 1.1 per cent reported Black, Asian, or mixed ethnicity, an under-representation as the 2001 census found that 2.0 per cent of the Scottish population were from ethnic minorities (Office of Chief Statistician, 2004). This has not been a problem confined to the SNP. Studies of other UK parties show that they have overwhelmingly white memberships (Whiteley et al., 1994; Whiteley and Seyd, 2002). Yet the SNP had made considerable effort to attract Asian Scots to vote and join the party in recent years. In 2007, Bashir Ahmad, SNP List Member for Glasgow, became the first Asian Member of the Scottish Parliament.

Many Scots acknowledge a religious identity, having been brought up in a religious tradition, but have abandoned the faith while retaining vestiges of that identity. Amongst SNP members, 57.4 per cent regard themselves as 'belonging to a religion'. Only 13 per cent (of the full sample) described themselves as 'very religious' compared to 32 per cent 'not very' and 8 per cent 'not at all', and only one in four attends services at least once a week compared to 31 per cent attending 'never or practically never'. Of those who identify with a religion, the figures for the SNP broadly reflect Scotland as a whole.

The SNP is similar to the Labour Party and very different from the Conservatives and Scottish Greens in terms of the proportion of religious members. However, when it comes to the denominational breakdown, and notably its ability to attract Catholics, the SNP is quite different from Labour. Despite the decline of religion, the Conservatives continue to be a largely Protestant party in Scotland (Curtice and Seawright, 1995). The reason for this is that the party fell back on its core support and was less able than Labour to appeal to voters beyond its core. Labour succeeded in holding onto, while expanding beyond, its core religious vote (Table 4.4).

Socio-economic background

Objective and subjective class status often diverge. An individual may feel working class, perhaps because of background, but objectively have the occupation, income, status, and wealth of being middle class. Many people reject an association with a social class and this can also be politically significant. Subjective class identity may compete or

Table 4.4. Religious identity and denomination of party memberships (%)

	SNP (2007–08)	Conservative (1992)	Liberal Democrats (1998–99)	Labour (1997) Overall	Labour (1997) Scottish only	Scottish Green (2002)	Population (2001 census)
Religion:							
Yes	57	89	65	56	57	34	67
No	43	11	15	44	43	66	33
N	*6638*	*2435*	*2866*	*5771*	*364*	*260*	
Of those saying yes:							
Church of Scotland/England	66	78	70	24	50	18	63
Catholic	18	8	11	57	43	9	24
Other Christian	11	12	15	14	4	48	10
Other	5	3	5	5	3	25	3

complement other identities, most notably national identity in Scotland. Before considering subjective class, it is important to consider the objective class composition of the SNP and how this relates to its members' attitudes towards class.

At the time of the survey, only 42 per cent were in full-time paid employment and a further 6 per cent were employed part-time. Most of the remainder were retired with only small proportions unemployed, permanently sick or disabled, looking after the home or in full-time education. The proportion of retired members was similar to that found in studies of the Conservative Party in 1992 and Liberal Democrats in 1998–99. Those not currently in work were requested to answer the occupational questions with reference to their most recent job. The familiar Goldthorpe classification of employment suggests a pattern very similar to that found in parties throughout Britain and beyond. There is little here that makes the SNP distinctive. The same is true when we look at the public/private sector breakdown of employment. While Labour members are disproportionately employed in the public sector and the converse is true of the Conservatives, the split amongst SNP members is about equal (Table 4.5).

Table 4.5. Goldthorpe social class, work sector among party memberships (%)

	SNP (2007–08)	Conservative (1992)	Liberal Democrats (1998–99)	Labour (1997)	
				Overall	Scottish only
Social class					
Salariat	61	55	74	64	59
Routine non-manual	17	18	11	12	12
Petty bourgeoisie	5	13	7	2	3
Foremen/ technicians	7	6	4	7	8
Working class	10	8	5	15	18
N	6885	2095	2866	5218	333
Sector					
Private company	46	60	38	37	39
Public sector	48	32	46	49	49
Charity/ voluntary	5	10	10	5	8
Other			5	9	4
N	6309	2082	2866	5019	320

Table 4.6. Annual income of SNP members

Annual income	%
Up to £10,000	13
£10,000–£20,000	24
£20,000–£30,000	20
£30,000–£40,000	14
£40,000–£50,000	9
£50,000–£60,000	7
Over £60,000	14
N	5470

The overall distribution of incomes in the SNP also looks similar to that in other parties. However, four in ten members are retired and likely to have incomes significantly below what they would have earned in real terms prior to retirement. When retired members are excluded from the analysis, the average household income rises to between £30,000 and £40,000 from between £20,000 and £30,000 (Table 4.6).

Education is closely related to social class, both as a reflection of social background and as an engine of social mobility. SNP members are generally relatively well educated. This is likely to become more pronounced over time: currently this is suppressed by the effects of age, with membership more common among generations educated before the era of mass higher education. The party has considerably fewer members with no educational qualifications compared with both the Conservatives and Labour (Table 4.7). Beyond this, the patterns are broadly similar across parties including the over-representation of graduates. Just over a third of SNP members have a degree, similar to Labour members in 1997 and smaller than the proportions found in the Greens and Liberal Democrats. These results parallel those with income. SNP

Table 4.7. Educational attainment of SNP members compared with other parties

	% members in full-time education	% members with a degree
SNP, 2007/08	2.5	35
Labour, 1997	2.8	34
Labour, 1989/90	3.0	29
Conservative, 1992	0.4	12
Liberal Democrats, 1998/99	2.0	42
Liberal Democrats, 1993	3.0	49
Scottish Green, 2002	16.8	74
Scottish Green, 1990	10.6	63
UK Greens, 1990	8.4	55

members, in common with other parties, are therefore better educated than the population as a whole, though not substantially so. A significant proportion of the membership has no qualifications from beyond the statutory schooling period placing the SNP alongside the 'traditional' parties rather than new social movement parties such as the Greens, which emerged in and from the era of mass higher education and are consequently dominated by graduates. More than half of SNP members had completed full-time education by the age of 17, and a very small number indicated they were currently students, similar to proportions found in other mainstream parties.

Subjective identities

SNP members are comparatively reluctant to assign themselves to a social class (Table 4.8). Only 43 per cent did so, compared to around two out of three members from each of the other parties for which data are available. Of those assigning themselves a class identity, the split between middle and working class was relatively even. Amongst Labour members in Scotland in 1997, almost three-quarters described themselves as working class. Respondents were also asked how they would describe their household's social-class status at the time of their birth. The responses point to considerable upward social mobility among the SNP membership. Of those reporting a working-class background (and also assigning themselves to a class), almost 40 per cent identified themselves as middle class and only 9 per cent of those with middle-class parents reported moving in the opposite direction (i.e. from a

Table 4.8. Extent and direction of class identity among party memberships (%)

	SNP (2007–08)	Conservative (1992)	Liberal Democrats (1998–99)	Labour (1997) Overall	Labour (1997) Scottish only
Belong to a class?					
Yes	43	62	67	66	70
No	57	38	33	34	30
N	*6638*	*2401*	*2866*	*5511*	*352*
Of those saying yes:					
Middle	54	82	82	42	27
Working	46	18	18	58	73

Practice varied across the surveys in terms of whether an 'other' option was offered or accepted if volunteered. To enable cleaner comparison, 'other' responses are excluded from Table 4.8.

middle-class background to working-class status now). Similar patterns have been found in studies of Conservative and Liberal Democrat members (Whiteley et al., 1994: 47; 2006: 25).

Geography and the SNP membership

A significant minority of SNP members (11 per cent) were born outside Scotland (Table 4.9) including 6.7 per cent who were born in England, a figure not far below the 8.1 per cent in Scotland's population recorded in the 2001 census. One possibility with those born outside Scotland, of course, is that they had Scottish parents or had some Scottish connection but circumstances, such as a parental employment, meant that they happened to be born outside Scotland. We therefore calculated, for each category in Table 4.9, the proportions of those members whose father was born in or outside Scotland. (In other words, the numbers in the right-hand part of the table are row percentages, as opposed to the column percentages that are the standard approach in this book.) Around one-third of those members born in England or outside the British Isles were born to a Scottish father. Nonetheless, that still leaves two-thirds, and thus around 7 per cent of the total membership, who were neither born in Scotland nor born to Scottish parents but are committed enough to the cause of Scottish nationalism to join the SNP.

A high proportion of SNP members (51 per cent) have lived outside Scotland for six months or more. This proportion drops only slightly to 46 per cent if we exclude from the calculations those who were actually born outside Scotland. Of those born in Scotland but resident for more than six months elsewhere, 48 per cent had lived in England, and only 4 per cent had lived elsewhere in the United Kingdom or Ireland, with the remaining 48 per cent having lived further afield. In Table 4.10, we show how these results breakdown by age and sex (again excluding those born outside Scotland). Among those of pensionable age, males are

Table 4.9. Birthplace and father's birthplace of SNP members (%)

	% of total	Father's birthplace		N
		Scotland	Elsewhere	
Scotland	89	92	8	6037
England	7	34	66	449
Wales/NI/Rep. of Ireland	1	16	84	65
Other	3	39	61	196
N	6821			

Table 4.10. Proportion of members that have lived outside Scotland for more than six months by age and sex (%)

	Aged 18–40		Aged 41–65		Aged 66+	
	Male	Female	Male	Female	Male	Female
Always lived in Scotland	66	64	55	66	39	62
Lived in England	16	14	25	14	26	19
Lived in Wales/NI/Rep. of Ireland	2	6	2	1	2	1
Lived elsewhere	16	16	18	19	33	18
N	*619*	*187*	*1987*	*891*	*1288*	*719*

markedly more likely to have lived not only outside Scotland but also outside the British Isles, probably reflecting the impact of the Second World War and national service. Among those in the middle-age category, males are again more likely to have lived outside Scotland, but this time England was the most likely destination. Those born in the late 1950s and early 1960s, and whose working lives therefore began during the first post-war period of mass unemployment, were the likeliest to have lived in England. Those in the youngest age group are the least likely to have lived outside Scotland, no doubt partly because they have had less time in which to do so. It is noticeable that the gender gap has closed within this group: females are as likely to have experience of living elsewhere. Once again, however, these patterns should not be over-interpreted. The key point is that a large proportion of SNP members have experience of life outside Scotland.

Next, we turn to where the members live. Only 4 per cent lived outside Scotland, mainly in England. Reflecting the points just made about emigration, three-quarters of these were born in Scotland. In Table 4.11, we exclude those who live outside Scotland and show the distribution of the remaining members among the eight Scottish Parliament electoral regions. To put these in context, the middle column shows the distribution of the SNP's 2007 regional list vote – that is, the proportion of its total vote that came from each region – and the right-hand column shows the regional distribution of the Scottish adult population as a whole. As these latter figures indicate, the Parliamentary regions are intended to be broadly similar in population size so that each, with the exception of the Highlands and Islands, contains around 13 per cent of the Scottish electorate. There are some marked contrasts between the distributions of votes and membership. Membership rates vary quite sharply. The south of Scotland, where the SNP came a close second to Labour in the 2007 list vote, provides just 4 per cent of the party's members. Meanwhile, the region supplying the largest

Table 4.11. Regional distribution of SNP members, SNP voters, and Scottish population

	% of membership	% of SNP vote (2007)	% of population (2007)
Northeast Scotland	17	17	13
South of Scotland	4	12	13
Lothians	18	12	13
Central Scotland	10	14	14
Glasgow	16	9	12
Highlands and Islands	10	10	9
West of Scotland	14	12	12
Mid Scotland and Fife	11	14	13

Table 4.12. Urban–rural residence of SNP members, SNP voters, and Scottish population

	% of membership	% of SNP vote (2007)	% of population (2007)
Big city	17	35	38
Suburbs/outskirt of big city	15	28	30
Small city/town	38	16	13
Country village	23	14	11
Farm/home in country	8	7	7

proportion of the membership is Lothians but this is not reflected in the party's regional vote share. Evidently, the relationship between electoral strength and membership is not straightforward.

Table 4.12 presents the same comparisons as in the previous table but this time on the basis of an urban–rural classification.[1] More than two-thirds of Scots live in urban areas, either cities or their outskirts but less than one in three SNP members live in urban Scotland. The SNP's membership is mainly to be found in small towns and villages. It is, then, reasonable to talk about the party's 'heartlands' but the notion is not best understood in terms of particular regions of Scotland. Rather, the party tends to recruit members disproportionately from the rural and semi-rural areas within most if not all of Scotland's regions.

---

[1] These are not exact comparisons because the electoral and population data are based on the Scottish Government's eightfold classification (see http://www.scotland.gov.uk/Publications/2008/07/29152642/9) whereas the survey respondents simply chose between the labels set out in the table. However, the two sets of categories map onto one another fairly closely, enabling broad comparison.

Conclusion

Perhaps the most noticeable feature of these results is precisely the lack of striking findings. The profile of SNP members is quite similar to that of most other parties, both in Britain and beyond; they are older, more male, better educated and more middle class than the adult population as a whole. The biggest contrast with other parties operating in Scotland tended to be with the Greens, suggesting that, at least in terms of membership, the SNP belongs more among what are called the 'major' parties than among the 'minor' or 'protest' parties. In the absence of comparable data from earlier years, we cannot tell whether this has long been true of the SNP, or whether it is a feature of the party's more professional and pragmatic approach since devolution.

As such, there are relatively few surprises in the analyses above. One or two of the findings stand out, however, usually because they conflict with the stereotypical impressions of the party formed during its rise to prominence in the 1970s. For example, the SNP is not a young people's party. It is a decidedly male party. It is a fairly secular party, though with significant numbers of religious adherents, but not one whose membership is confined to its electoral heartlands of the north and east. Most noticeably of all, the SNP does not have an insular membership whose interests stretch no further than Scotland's borders. Half of the members were either born outside Scotland or have since lived outside the country for a significant period of time.

5

Membership Motivations

Introduction

This chapter examines motivations for joining the Scottish National Party (SNP) based on an analysis of members' self-declared reasons for joining. The approach differs from other studies of motivation in that instead of asking members to choose from a list of possible reasons, this study involved a simple open-ended question, 'Thinking back to your first decision to join the party, what were the main reasons that you joined the party?' This approach produces far more information and requires care in coding the 6,290 answers ranging from simply 'Independence' to lengthy accounts of when, how, and why a member joined. However, the advantage is that we have allowed the members themselves to tell us why they joined rather than imposing our own theoretical explanations on them. In the case of the SNP, the range of answers was limited by the party's clear and relatively unambiguous definition of its aims. Unlike a number of other parties, the SNP has an objective that is reasonably easily identified. However, while independence is the main reason people join the party, this is not the entire story and it is possible to relate motivations for joining the party to the growing body of literature on the subject of motivations for political participation.

Established theories of participation suggest that members require incentives to participate. However, at least five identifiable approaches to understanding political mobilization exist. The first type comprises resource-based approaches and civic voluntarism (Verba et al., 1995). These focus on the socio-economic status and cognitive resources of participants or on 'having the resources to act'. Previous studies have revealed that party members are socio-economically well off. As the previous chapter showed, the SNP is consistent with this pattern (see also Mitchell et al., 2009). However, identifying the social background characteristics and cognitive resources of members simply draws attention to the 'types' of people likely to participate. It does not explain cognitive processes at work in the individual's decision to join. In other words, motivations cannot be inferred from socio-demographic variables (see Achen, 1992).

The second broad theoretical approach, rational choice, is more helpful in this regard. From Olson (1965) to 'expanded' concepts of rationality, the emphasis is on selective and collective incentives behind membership. The central argument is that individuals join parties and become active in response to incentives, thus overcoming the costs of participation. This approach has informed many studies of parties, and most of these conclude that policy and ideology (collective incentives) are supremely important, thus challenging Olson's claim that collective incentives do not sufficiently explain mobilization. Wilson (1995: 96), for example, points to 'purpose, principle, and ideology'. However, researchers have worked with various different categories of incentives. An influential categorization is provided by Clarke and Wilson (1961) who refer to material (tangible rewards of membership), solidary (derived from social interaction), and purposive (the goals of the organization) incentives.

Mobilization/organizational approaches accept the rational choice assumptions but place more emphasis on efforts made by the organization to attract members, the idea being that opinion and discontent must be organized, that is, individuals are drawn into membership through the recruitment efforts of the organization. Amongst studies of interest groups, it is not uncommon to claim that 'collective interests do not explain group membership – recruitment activity does' (Johnson, 1998: 60). In the context of political parties, less weight is attached to such explanations as parties are more clearly associated with the pursuit of collective aims but recruitment strategies may be of some relevance as all parties make some attempt to attract new members. Another consideration in this literature is the existence of organizational recruitment networks – when belonging to one organization exposes the individual to the recruitment efforts of others.

The most influential approach in recent studies of parties in Britain is the general incentives model. Developed by Whiteley and Seyd, and described as the coming together of rational choice and social–psychological perspectives on participation (Whiteley and Seyd, 2002: 93), the model accepts the existence of various selective and collective incentives but identifies other motivations which 'operate within a fundamentally different type of discourse than cost–benefit analysis', namely altruism, expressive attachments, and social norms (Seyd and Whiteley, 1992: 63). The authors have modified their model over the years and some of the classifications are debatable; for example, ideology is now regarded as a selective incentive and a belief in ideological principles was previously categorized as altruism (see Seyd and Whiteley, 1992: 4). However, the basic premise that participation involves a complex mix of collective and selective incentives, and cost–benefit assessments as well as more emotionally based responses is widely accepted. The most recent manifestation of the general incentives model uses 'five distinct factors' to explain why people join a party or become active in a party (3, 4, and 5 existing outside the rational choice cost–benefit framework of analysis) (Whiteley et al., 2006: 76–82):

1. *Selective incentives*

   a. *Selective outcome*: private benefits gained from participation, e.g., wanting to be a councillor; viewing membership as good for career.

   b. *Selective process*: satisfaction/entertainment gained from being part of the process of politics. 'For some people, the political process is interesting and stimulating in itself, regardless of outcome or goals.' Only members can experience this enjoyment.

   c. *Ideological*: 'the process of sharing values and beliefs with other people' – similar to churchgoers.

2. *Collective incentives (policy goals)*

   a. *Positive*: the pursuit of public goods (party policies).

   b. *Negative*: the reduction of a public bad (other parties' policies).

3. *Altruism*

   A sense of duty to participate or moral imperative such as a desire to create a more compassionate society, rather than a specific policy goal.

4. *Affective/expressive/emotional motives*

   These motives for joining are 'grounded in a sense of loyalty and affection for the party that is unrelated to cognitive calculations of costs and benefits'.

5. *Social norms*

   A desire to win approval of others.

A fifth broad approach to participation considers political activity within its context or institutional setting. Some accounts of participation in parties and other political organizations consider the context in which decisions are made to be crucial. Attention is paid to macropolitical factors and how these might influence cost–benefit calculations of the individual. Some social movement studies, namely political opportunity structure approaches, are illustrative (Kitschelt, 1986;

McAdam 1996). A recent addition to the literature on political participation (Morales, 2009) also takes this position, exploring the links between individual- and context-level factors, including the suggestion that decentralization of government structures may provide incentives for political participation. Thus, the focus of attention shifts to the political context or setting in which the decision to join is taken. In the case of the SNP, for example, a member may have been persuaded to join in light of devolution or in response to the party entering government. Understanding the political context, therefore, may be important in explaining political mobilization.

This chapter examines specific reasons for joining the SNP. We first provide an account of the real-life explanations provided by SNP members in response to the open-ended question. Then we attempt to categorize the responses drawing on the above literature. Finally, we explore the link between motivations and the time period during which members joined.

Self-declared reasons for joining the SNP

The respondents had the opportunity to describe a number of motivations for joining, that is, multiple reasons were possible. In total, 88.4 per cent of all respondents provided a written account of why they joined the party. In most cases, more than one reason was given (Table 5.1). It was not always possible to determine the relative importance of reasons given.[1]

Table 5.1. Responses to question on why joined

Number of reasons given	N	% of all respondents
0	822	11.6
1	2151	30.2
2	2913	41.0
3	900	12.7
4	272	3.8
5	54	0.8
	7112	*100*

[1] As the relative importance of the stated reasons could seldom be inferred from the information provided, reasons for joining were coded as '1st reason', '2nd reason', and so on according to the order in which the statements were given.

Table 5.2. Reported reasons for joining the SNP (%)

	First stated reason	All stated reasons
Independence	44.3	55.7
General liking for party	9.6	14.5
Anti-union/Scotland talked down	7.0	13.3
Further Scottish interests	6.4	10.2
Dislike other parties	5.0	8.9
Family/social links	4.6	6.4
Participation	3.9	8.5
Scottish/national identity	3.0	4.1
General reference to Scotland/Scotland as a nation	2.9	6.2
Past event/period	2.5	5.8
Personal circumstances	2.5	3.7
Party contact	2.0	3.4
Devolution	1.3	1.7
Leaders	1.3	2.8
Issues	1.1	4.7
Ideology[a]	0.3	0.8
Material rewards	0.1	0.2
Other/unclear	2.4	6.1
N	6290	

[a] By this, we mean ideological principles other than nationalism/belief in independence, for example, belief in social democracy or social justice.

The initial results of the question on reasons for joining are reported in Table 5.2.[2] To reiterate, these are reasons for joining as described by the members in their own words. Data in the first column derive from the first stated reason for joining, those in the second column are based on the multiple responses (and so the percentages sum to more than 100). Political attitudes are the main reasons for joining the SNP. By far the most commonly cited reason is a belief in independence. Over half of our respondents referred to the SNP's primary objective as stated in the party's constitution. One-tenth referred to a desire to promote or further Scottish interests, to 'stand up for Scotland', the other official objective of the SNP. This is the second aim of the SNP as stated in the party's constitution. Another 6 per cent made a more general reference to Scotland and/or perceived national attributes – Scotland's economy, history, or culture. A less specific explanation, a general liking for the

---

[2] Although coding requires the enforcement of distinct categories, it is clear that there is substantial overlap or at least interrelationship between many of those listed in Table 5.2. This is an unavoidable problem in the quantification of qualitative data and it means that the results should probably be regarded as indicative rather than precise. Nonetheless, by the yardsticks of standard inter- and intra-coder tests, these codings are at least highly reliable. Two coders, classifying a sample of reasons from 200 respondents, chose the same category for 91 per cent of reasons.

SNP, was offered by around 15 per cent of respondents. Almost one in ten expressed a desire to contribute to the cause or to be actively involved, referred to as 'participation' in the table, though this may be an indirect way of referring to the party's objectives. Very few of the responses contained specific reference to the importance of Scottish national identity. Taken together, many of those who do not cite independence instead mention motivations that amount to seeing the SNP as in some way good for Scotland. In essence, SNP members are joining a party for reasons that conform with the party's own stated aims.

A negative expression of motivation for joining involved a critique of the union and how Scotland has fared being part of it, cited by 13 per cent of respondents. A sizeable number referred to Scotland being 'swallowed up' or economically 'worse off' because of Westminster/London rule; others focused on a lack of democratic accountability or legitimacy, for example, 'decisions made in England for Scotland' and what some referred to as a 'democratic deficit'. Explicit anti-English sentiment was almost nowhere to be seen. Only 0.4 per cent of respondents were classified as making anti-English statements, not dissimilar to the proportion of respondents who oppose the existence of any Scottish Parliament. More common was criticism of other political parties with almost 10 per cent expressing a dislike for other parties, especially the Labour Party.

A significant number of members point to the importance of issues or policies other than independence promoted by the party such as the removal of nuclear weapons, education, or local taxation policy. However, at 5 per cent of total responses, these are dwarfed by those who identify independence as their main motivation. A similar proportion of respondents refer to a past event or period in Scottish political history which influenced their decision to join. The most often cited events, in descending order of importance, were the discovery of 'Scotland's oil', 'Thatcherism', the 1979 devolution referendum, the Iraq war, the Hamilton by-election of 1967, the poll tax, and the 2007 Scottish Parliament elections. Devolution is presented separately in the table, and it is notable that few refer to devolution or the creation of the Scottish Parliament as an inspiration for joining – a smaller number than the combined total of members who point to Thatcherism or the poll tax.

Slightly more than one in twenty members identify networks as being influential – being persuaded to join by a family member, friend, or colleague, joining because of social benefits, or becoming involved through the membership of other organizations. Other influences listed in the table appear relatively unimportant. A small number of members refer to party leaders or senior figures in the party as being important in their decision to join. Party campaigns or recruitment attempts do not feature prominently. Finally, material rewards for membership are extremely low-ranking, which is consistent with the studies of other parties in Britain.

A theme that emerges is the blurred distinction between 'why' and 'how' members join a political party. The mechanics of joining, or *how* members join (whether through a local party, national HQ, through a party canvasser, and so on), are often conflated with reasons *why* they joined. It is probable that in some cases the SNP respondents conflate these processes, demonstrating the interrelatedness in people's minds of the reasons for joining and the mechanisms through which they join.

Categorizing membership motivation

As argued above, the dominant approach in the study of members' motivations for joining parties is incentives-based but this is by no means the only approach to understanding political involvement. On the basis of the various approaches evident in the motivations literature, reasons for joining the SNP can be categorized under the following broad headings:

1. *Selective material incentives*: career or financial benefits.

2. *Selective process incentives*: a desire to become active in politics.

3. *Collective/purposive incentives (independence)*: clearly expressed support for the SNP's core policy of independence.

4. *Collective/purposive incentives (other)*: other policies/issues promoted by the party, the party's other ideological principles, or a negative account of the impact of other parties/policies on Scotland. In this category, we include commitments to nationalism and references to Scotland being 'different'.

5. *Expressive motives*: a more general expression of support for the party, rather than a specific commitment to political goals. Examples include 'I wanted to support the cause'.

6. *Social influences and networks*: reference to social networks (family/ friends/colleagues/other group members involved in party) being influential in the decision to join, and/or social benefits gained from membership.

7. *Party mobilization (recruitment)*: being persuaded to join by party-related behaviour, such as canvassing, a poster, party broadcast, or being asked to join by a politician.

8. *Party mobilization (leaders)*: included here are references to the party leadership or senior figures in the party, for example, Salmond being viewed as a good/inspirational leader.

9. *Political context*: including various political events which may have triggered joining, for example, Thatcherism, the poll tax, devolution, or the party's recent electoral success.

10. *Personal circumstances*: examples include experience of living abroad or other life event.

11. *Other/unclear*.

Using this classification, the members' reasons for joining were categorized as outlined in Table 5.3. The data confirm the importance of collective goals and, most strikingly, the aim of independence. Independence is by far the most common explanation offered amongst first stated reasons. However, it is quite striking that when multiple reasons are considered, other collective incentives also come to prominence. Many of the members expanded on their initial account of independence as a motivation for joining but did so with other collectively based explanations. Beyond these collective motives, expressive incentives – general statements of support for the party – appear the next most important reasons for joining the SNP. It is also notable that significant minorities of members mentioned political context and selective process incentives, where the members indicated a desire to become involved in politics. Party mobilization factors remain relatively unimportant and selective material processes barely register in this analysis, confirming that party members account for their joining in very different terms from those often used by researchers to explain those decisions.

Table 5.3. Motivations categories (%)

	First stated reason	All stated reasons
Selective material	0.1	0.2
Selective process	2.9	6.8
Collective – independence	44.3	55.7
Collective – other	26.8	40.1
Expressive	9.1	13.1
Networks	4.6	6.4
Party mobilization – recruitment	2.0	3.4
Party mobilization – leaders	1.3	2.8
Political context	4.0	7.9
Personal circumstances	2.5	3.7
Other/unclear	2.4	6.1
N	*6290*	

Approximately one in twenty respondents indicated that social or network influences were important in joining. In other party studies in Britain, this figure has ranged from 4 per cent in the case of the Liberal Democrats (Whiteley et al., 2006: 87) to 12 per cent for the Conservatives (Whiteley et al., 1994: 97). On the face of it, then, SNP members do not appear to be especially influenced by family or friends.

However, it would be misleading to conclude that these party members are not involved in networks. Large numbers report being members of a trade union either now or in the past (56 per cent), or a professional association (38 per cent). The next most popular form of organizational involvement is a church or religious group with more than four in every ten of our respondents reporting taking part either now or in the past. Beyond this, the members report rather high levels of involvement in arts, music, cultural, and sports-related groups, with around a third having been members of such groups. Perhaps even more interesting is the level of participation in voluntary or charity groups, organizations commonly assumed to pursue public goods, that is, public interest rather than self-interest. Nearly 30 per cent report being involved in youth work; the same number in a conservation group (e.g. the National Trust); around one in five report being involved in a local community action group; 18 per cent have at some point been associated with a group helping the elderly or disabled (e.g. Help the Aged); and 13.5 per cent have previously been members of another party. This high figure for previous party membership reflects the SNP's relative newness as a significant force in Scottish politics. On average, members reported belonging to 1.8 organizations in addition to their party membeship. According to this evidence, SNP members are well-networked suggesting that the party remains the rooted, connected party it was in the 1960s (Schwarz, 1970; Mansbach, 1973).

Motivations and time of joining

Motivations for joining a party may vary according to the time of joining. The 'context-based' literature suggests that those who join a political organization during a period of objective 'success' are likely to have different motivations from those who join the cause at a time of relative difficulty or unpopularity. Generally speaking, the former are more likely to have a shallow commitment to the cause while the latter are more strongly ideological. In the context of Scottish politics, the SNP's recent rise to government can be contrasted with periods in the party's history when it struggled to have an impact electorally (see

Chapter 2). Against this backdrop, we are interested in whether those who joined the party most recently are distinct in their reasons for joining.

Overall, roughly a third of members first joined in or after 2000, a third between 1980 and 1999, and the others in the 1970s or before. Table 5.4 breaks this down according to key dates in the party's development, as outlined in earlier chapters. This is by no means a party of brand new members and appears not untypical when compared with the proportion of new members in other parties, defined as those who joined in the three-year period leading up to the respective surveys (Table 5.5).

The SNP's electoral success in 2007 appears to have encouraged former members to return to the party. Almost one-fifth of the members at the time of our survey were 'returners', that is, they had allowed their membership to lapse and had returned to the party. This figure is high when compared with other studies. Table 5.6 looks in greater detail at when these returning members came back to the party. The majority of returners rejoined following the creation of the Scottish Parliament, a large number since 2005, and nearly one in four in 2007, the year of the party's electoral success, whether before or after the election. The vast majority of returners had first joined the party many years ago,

Table 5.4. Time period first joined (%)

1930–66	12.1
1967–73	12.3
1974–79	9.5
1980–88	10.2
1989–2000	22.7
2001–04	8.3
2005 or later	24.9
N	*6572*

Table 5.5. New members (% joining for first time in three years before survey) and returning members

	New members (%)	Returning members (%)
SNP	24.9	18.7
Conservative, 1992	12.2	8.2
Green (British), 2002	26.8	14.9
Green (Scottish), 1990	61.4	20.3
Green (Scottish), 2002	43.4	9.9
Liberal Democrats, 1993	27.2	–
Labour, 1989/90	14.1	14.9
Labour, 1997	33.6	14.5

Table 5.6. If returners, year last rejoined (%)

Year last rejoined			
1930–66			0.8
1967–73			2.1
1974–79			2.6
1980–88			9.4
1989–2000			23.2
2001–04			15.3
2005 or later			46.6
	2005	10.9	
	2006	11.5	
	2007/08	24.2	
N			1170

including 22.4 per cent before 1967. Looking at those who had returned to the party from 2005 onwards, 48 per cent had initially joined before 1980 partly accounting for the party's age profile. Since 2005, then, the party has attracted many former members, a large number of whom first joined some decades ago.

We can also assess the proportion of incoming members for each period who have returned to the party (Table 5.7). This analysis reveals that since 2001, one-third of those entering the party have been re-joiners. The numbers returning to the party are no doubt partly a function of the popularity of the party at the time of the survey but it may also be related to the organizational changes within the party. Prior to 2004, the branch structure resulted in a large number of members 'drifting away' from the party. Party officials reported losing around 1,000 members a year in this way, described by one official as 'mainly folk who just weren't signed up again'. In other words, some would have made a conscious decision to leave, others might have died or moved away from the local branch area and, for a large number, membership would have lapsed because of inactivity at the branch level. The party has concentrated on retaining members once they join rather than

Table 5.7. Proportion of new and returning members by time period (%)

	New members	Returning members
1930–66	98.9	1.1
1967–73	96.9	3.1
1974–79	95.1	4.9
1980–88	83.6	16.4
1989–2000	81.8	18.2
2001–04	67.2	32.8
2005+	66.7	33.3

pursuing former members but it is clear that the membership in 2007/08 contained a large number of these returning members.

It is plausible that different groups in the party may be subject to different influences, depending on when they first joined or whether they are returners. It is reasonable to assume, for instance, that new members may have been inspired by a bandwagon effect. Returning members, on the other hand, might have a deeper commitment to independence even if this commitment has been tested during years when the SNP failed to advance electorally, leading to disillusionment and members drifting away. Table 5.8 begins to address this by comparing reported reasons for joining amongst new members and returning members (those who report discontinuity in membership).

Members who first joined in or after 2005 are considerably less likely to cite independence as a reason for joining while returning members are those most committed to the policy at the time of first joining or, at least,

Table 5.8. Reported reasons for joining the SNP, new members and returning members (all stated reasons) (%)

	New members since 1999	New members since 2005	Returners	Returned since 2005
Independence	51.4	48.3	63.2	63.9
General liking for party	22.7	24.5	10.6	13.1
Anti-union/Scotland talked down	8.1	7.7	15.0	14.3
Further Scottish interests	12.5	12.9	9.2	10.2
Dislike other parties	11.4	12.7	5.8	8.2
Family/social links	5.1	4.3	6.0	6.2
Participation	14.7	16.5	5.6	5.8
Scottish/national identity	2.3	1.8	5.4	5.2
General reference to Scotland/Scotland a nation	4.0	4.0	8.0	6.4
Past event/period	4.7	5.5	5.4	4.8
Personal circumstances	3.5	3.7	3.1	3.2
Party contact	3.0	2.8	3.0	2.2
Devolution	1.5	1.1	1.9	2.0
Leaders	5.8	7.3	1.1	1.0
Issues	5.7	7.0	3.8	2.0
Ideology	0.7	0.7	0.9	0.8
Material rewards	0.4	0.2	0.2	0.2
Other/unclear	6.1	7.1	6.4	5.8
N	2282	1514	1157	502

those who have given the policy as the reason for first joining. However, even amongst its most recent recruits, independence is by far the main reason for joining the SNP. New members are also less likely to offer negative statements on Scotland's place within the Union or to refer to a sense of nationalism. Conversely, the new members are more likely to declare a general liking for the party, to point to a furthering of Scottish interests, and to suggest a desire for involvement. They are also more likely to indicate dislike of other parties as well as being considerably more likely to point to the influence of party leaders. In the vast majority of these cases, Alex Salmond was the leader identified as having an impact on their decision to join.

These findings suggest that the time period and political context are important in explaining why members join a party. Addressing this relationship in a slightly different way, Table 5.9 examines time joined and the categories of motivations used in Table 5.3. Of all cohorts, the most likely to refer to independence is the group joining between 1980 and 1988. This group is also most likely to mention the political context at the time they joined the party. The most frequent responses refer to Margaret Thatcher as Prime Minister, followed by the 1979 devolution referendum, North Sea oil, and the poll tax. Those joining between 1974 and 1979 are also quite inclined to cite contextual influences, most commonly the events surrounding the 1979 referendum and the debate over 'Scotland's oil'. This suggests groups of members politicized by the events of the day.

Table 5.9. Motivations by time period joined (multiple responses) (%)

	1930–66	1967–73	1974–79	1980–88	1989–2000	2001–04	2005–08
Selective material		0.1	0.2		0.3	0.6	0.2
Selective process	1.8	3.4	3.9	3.1	6.5	10.2	13.1
Collective independence	55.5	55.7	56.6	61.9	60.3	55.9	48.3
Collective other	43.3	42.0	40.2	41.3	40.9	36.3	40.6
Expressive	4.3	4.5	8.5	6.6	13.7	20.0	23.6
Networks	6.8	8.8	7.4	7.6	5.9	6.8	4.3
Party mobilization recruitment	4.1	4.5	4.6	1.8	3.2	3.2	2.8
Party mobilization leaders	1.3	0.4	0.7	0.8	1.7	3.0	7.3
Political context	4.8	8.4	12.6	13.2	6.6	5.0	7.5
Personal circumstances	4.3	4.0	7.1	2.9	2.8	3.2	3.7
N	704	729	564	622	1387	499	1514

Though independence remains the overwhelming motivation for joining, the pattern emerging suggests that those who joined the SNP since 2005 are inspired to a greater extent by a desire to express support for the party or to be involved in politics rather than a strict adherence to independence than those who joined earlier. However, this should not be exaggerated as independence is by far the most important reason for joining for all cohorts of members and is only relatively less important amongst recent joiners compared with previous generations. The less conspicuous devotion to independence amongst new members may partly be the result of a form of socialization which takes place within the party, that is, with the passage of time members develop an independence-focused perspective. However, it is also possible that these members are simply more pragmatic in their approach to constitutional issues, reflecting the wider political strategy of the party. Some may even oppose independence, having been attracted to the party for reasons other than its constitutional stance.

There is also a suggestion that the new members are more open to leadership influences. This does not necessarily suggest that these members have a shallow commitment to the party or that this is jumping on a bandwagon of electoral success. However, we can conclude that the new members offer a more diverse range of explanations for joining, beyond a commitment to independence.

Conclusion

In this chapter, we have examined SNP members' self-reported motivations for joining the party. Most previous studies have adopted a different approach from that used here. While acknowledging the difficulties coding the large number of (sometimes lengthy) responses, this proved useful and allowed the members to answer the question in their own words. This was not an attempt to test resource-based or rational choice models of membership: we neither expected nor received responses like 'I'm quite well educated and I had a lot of time on my hands' or 'because the likely benefits outweighed the limited membership fee'. Rather, we sought to move beyond these approaches and to identify which of the range of general incentives seemed to have been important motivations for SNP members. In particular, we could assess whether, as in previous studies (using a different method), collective/purposive incentives dominated members' thinking. The short answer is that they did, with the SNP's core policy objective of independence being mentioned by 56 per cent of members.

However, while independence is clearly a strong driver of SNP membership, not all respondents felt obliged to mention it. The next most common category of motivations was 'collective – other', which included support for the party's other policies, general ideological principles, and in particular its commitment to Scottish interests. The key point about these reasons is that they are party-specific. It is unlikely that these members would have joined a different party even if it offered greater material benefits or better opportunities to participate. This point sounds obvious but can be lost in studies focused on the resources available to or the costs and benefits facing members. These are not considerations uppermost in people's minds when deciding to join a party.

Our results contribute to the growing literature on other factors, including networks, context-specific circumstances, and leadership influences in generating political participation. These have provided an impetus for joining the SNP and are much more successful than party efforts at national recruitment campaigns. Again, the limitations of generalized resource-based and cost–benefit approaches are clear. It is situational influences that translate the commitment to the SNP's politics into membership of the party. All in all, the importance of specific political commitment to the party is plain, and this is made doubly clear by the perceptible shifts in membership motivations over time. As the party has emphasized its pragmatism on the constitutional question and sought to broaden its support base with a view to winning office in the devolved arena, it has increasingly recruited members who are less committed to independence and more attracted by other features of the party's programme, image, and leadership.

6

Activism in the SNP

In this chapter, we address the nature of Scottish National Party (SNP) activism, sometimes referred to as intra-party participation. Historically, the SNP has been portrayed as a party with energetic grass roots, suggesting a large activist base highly involved in on-the-ground electoral campaigning and internal party decision-making (Brand, 1978). This image of the SNP derives from its role as an oppositional, extra-Parliamentary party in the days before devolution (Mitchell, 2009b). However, very little was actually known about patterns of activity within the party. Moreover, as the SNP secured its status as a Parliamentary party after devolution, alongside the organizational reforms discussed in Chapter 3, it moved from amateur activism towards a more electoral-professional type of party.

Previous research on political parties in Western democracies and elsewhere has consistently pointed to a decline in both membership numbers and activity rates of those who join parties (Katz and Mair, 1995; Dalton and Wattenberg, 2000; Mair and Van Beizen, 2001; Seyd and Whiteley, 2002; *Party Politics* special edition, 2004; Whiteley, 2009). Explanations for the decline in intra-party participation involve both the professionalization of parties and societal change (Dalton and Wattenberg, 2000; Whiteley, 2009). Some portray these trends as convenient for party leaders, as activists are assumed to be more radical in terms of policy and strategy than either passive members or leaders (May, 1973; Kitschelt, 1994). A large body of literature has emerged to defend the importance of grass-roots activists to parties. Activists are seen to perform crucial roles in the maintenance of party organizations by contributing to policy ideas and candidate and leadership selection, whilst also themselves providing a pool of potential candidates for public office. It is also argued that activists are integral to election campaigning and generally reaching out to the electorate. These internal and external functions are cited as evidence that parties need activists and ignore members at their cost (Scarrow, 1996; Denver et al., 2004; Marsh, 2004; Fisher and Denver, 2009).

Past studies of activism alert us to the complexity of membership participation. Members may be completely passive, never attending a local party event, or they may be intensely participative, never missing one. A broad distinction can be made between passive 'armchair' supporters and activists who commit time, money, and energy to their party. However, most members lie somewhere between these positions. Activism can also take many forms, from helping at a local fund-raising event to attending national party conference as a delegate. Previous studies of parties have identified at least three types of activities: internal or intra-party participation; election-related activities; and involvement in other (non-party) groups. Cross and Young (2008), in their study of young party members in Canada, refer to these as intra-party democracy, campaign activism and associational activism. Gallagher and Marsh (2002) use the terms internal, external (campaigning), and external (other activities in the community). Internal activities are those which involve participation in the party organization. These activities can appear procedural, rather than strictly political and focus on maintenance of party organization. They describe this as the party organization 'talking to itself' (Ibid.: 81). The other forms of activity involve members engaging with the wider community. Election activities can involve a range of campaign-centred tasks, from displaying party posters in windows to delivering leaflets and canvassing. Activism may be intermittent, with activities occurring, or intensifying, during key points in the election cycle. Party members may also be active within the community in other ways, through involvement in non-party organizations from local community groups to trade unions and church or religious groups. Through these contributions, party members perform the role of 'ambassadors in the community' (Scarrow, 1996: 43) and more generally contribute to party–society linkages (Seyd and Whiteley, 1992; Katz and Mair, 1995; Dalton and Wattenberg, 2000; Whiteley, 2009). These forms of activism are likely to be interrelated – for example, party meetings will include planning for election campaigns.

This chapter will explore the patterns of activism in the SNP with this multidimensional nature of activism in mind. We begin with an analysis of how we understand and measure activism, before exploring the various forms and dimensions of activity in the party and the determinants of activism. Finally, we consider the views of activists in the SNP and investigate whether they are more (or less) radical on policy and strategy than other groups.

What is activism?

Before we examine the structure and dimensions of participation in the SNP, we first explore some of the basic indicators of levels of activism in the party (Table 6.1). One-third of the SNP members indicate that they attend local meetings at least every few months. In answer to a question on self-perceived levels of activism, one-third of members describe themselves as fairly or very active, 40 per cent as not very active and 27 per cent as not at all active. The SNP members' perceptions of what it means to be active or inactive appear to be quite firmly based on attendance at local party meetings along with hours devoted to party activities per month. In other words, there is a high correlation between self-reported levels of activity and whether or not members attend meetings and devote time to the party: 83 per cent of those who consider themselves very active attend local meetings every month, but only 39 per cent of those who consider themselves fairly active attend so frequently.

Comparisons with other party membership studies in Britain suggest the SNP enjoys the benefits of a relatively active membership. SNP members tend to perceive themselves as rather active, and they are more likely to attend local party meetings. Table 6.2 compares data on members' self-perceptions of activism and here we see that SNP members are more likely to report they are active than Green, Liberal

Table 6.1. Basic indicators of activism

How active in the party	%	How often attend local meetings	%
Very active	11.6	Every month	19.4
Fairly active	21.3	Every few months	15.0
Not very active	39.8	About once a year	12.6
Not at all active	27.2	Less often	16.7
		Never	36.3
N	*6878*	*N*	*6837*

Table 6.2. Parties and self-reported activism (%)

	Fairly/very active	Not at all active
SNP	32.9	27.2
Scottish Greens, 2002	22.5	44.7
Liberal Democrats, 1999	30.0	29.0
Labour, 1997	27.0	31.0
Cons, 1992	20.0	45.0

Democrat, Conservative, or Labour members. While 36 per cent of the SNP respondents state that they never attend local meetings, in all other studies this proportion exceeds one in two members.[1]

However, basic measures of activism reveal little about the patterns of membership involvement. To provide a more accurate picture we assess activism in the SNP in a number of ways. The first of these is to construct an activism index, based on equal weighting of responses to four questions: self-perception; how often members attend meetings; time devoted to the party on average each month; and annual financial contributions. Most members devote no time at all to the party in the average month, while 21 per cent say they spend 1–2 hours on party activities; 15.5 per cent between 2 and 10 hours; and 6.4 per cent 10 hours or more. Members contribute on average £40.00 to the local party and £44.00 to the party nationally. Respondents are clustered towards the less active end of this dimension. If we split the index at equal intervals so as to divide respondents into five groups, there is a fairly steady decline in the numbers of respondents in each category as the level of activity increases (Figure 6.1). Hence the largest group, accounting for 39 per cent of respondents, is the least active. Nonetheless, that does mean that a majority of SNP members are at least somewhat, if only occasionally, active with most falling into the intermediate categories.

It might be argued that making financial contributions to a party is not activism as it does not involve time-commitment or interaction with others and looks rather more like 'armchair participation', or involvement from a distance, akin to the 'chequebook participation' identified in studies of pressure groups (Jordan and Maloney, 1997, 2007; Maloney, 2009). These scholars suggest that many supporters of groups do not perceive their financial commitment as political activism (Maloney, 2009: 280). If we recalculate the activity index, this time excluding the financial donations question, a rather different pattern emerges. This is shown by the lighter columns in Figure 6.1 with 48 per cent in the least active category. There is therefore a sizeable group of armchair members whose activity is confined to financial support.

[1] The SNP survey question asked how often members 'normally' attend local meetings, while the other studies asked about the 'last twelve months', that is, slightly different categories were used. However, we can compare 'Never/Not at all' data: SNP, 36 per cent; Scottish Greens Party 2002, 53 per cent; Liberal Democrats 1999, 53 per cent; Labour 1997, 54.0 per cent; Conservative, 66.0 per cent.

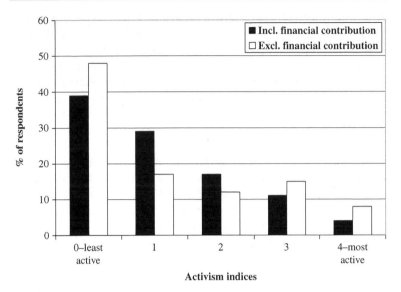

Figure 6.1. Distribution of respondents on activism indices (including and excluding financial contributions)

Forms and dimensions of activism

We can also examine activities undertaken over a longer time period and this too suggests that most members have been rather inactive. Table 6.3 shows the frequency with which respondents reported undertaking various party activities in the previous five years, and 'not at all' is the

Table 6.3. Activities on behalf of party in last five years (%)

	Very often	Fairly often	Not very often	Not at all
Displayed an election poster	40.6	18.7	13.3	27.4
Stood for office in the party	8.6	5.0	8.8	80.5
Attended a national party conference	12.2	8.8	13.6	65.3
Delivered leaflets during an election	32.4	13.8	13.1	40.7
Delivered leaflets between elections	17.2	11.3	15.8	55.7
Helped at a party function or with fundraising	16.7	14.8	19.6	48.9
Attended a party meeting	21.4	13.9	28.6	36.2
Canvassed voters door-to-door	13.4	9.2	13.6	63.8
Canvassed voters by telephone	5.4	4.9	10.3	79.3

largest response in all but one case. The exception, and the most common type of activity reported in the five years leading up to the survey, is displaying a party election poster. Previous studies have tended to view such activity as 'low cost' as it involves a minimal commitment of time (Whiteley et al., 1994: 102). However, this is a very public statement of support for a political party. Six in every ten SNP members had displayed a poster very or fairly often. This figure is close to that reported in the study of the Labour Party in 1990 when 65 per cent of members claimed to have 'frequently' displayed an election poster in a window, and considerably higher than that of other studies. In 2002, approximately half of all Scottish Green respondents indicated they had not done this at all, a similar figure to the British Conservatives in 1992.

The other election-related activity to stand out is delivering leaflets, with a third of members indicating they have done so 'very often' but a majority stating they had leafleted at least fairly often. More than one-fifth of the members have canvassed voters on the doorstep very or fairly often; a rather smaller proportion has done so by telephone. No other party membership study in Britain has recorded such high levels of door-to-door canvassing. This also applies to telephone canvassing: 19.7 per cent of SNP members had been involved in telephone canvassing compared with less than 10 per cent in all other party studies. This reflects the changing nature of campaigning and, in particular, the SNP's shift to telephone canvassing in the run-up to 2007.

The data suggest that the SNP is able to mobilize large numbers of activists for important elections. More members delivered leaflets during an election than attended meetings, suggesting that many are mobilized during elections but are less involved in the internal politics of party meetings. While standing for office in the party appeals only to a minority of members, over 30 per cent are prepared to help out at local functions and fundraising events, and almost one-fifth of the members say they have been to a national party conference, a time-intensive, high-cost activity.

Additionally, the survey reveals large numbers of local level elite-type activities: 18 per cent of the respondents had been a candidate for the party, mostly for local government; 30 per cent have been a branch office-bearer (e.g. convener, secretary, treasurer); and 14 per cent a constituency office-bearer. Whilst we also asked if members had held national positions, such as membership of the National Executive Committee (NEC) or national council, the survey data inevitably contains only small numbers who have done so (e.g. 2 per cent ($N = 134$) had been on the NEC). However, one in twenty respondents had served as a councillor. The evidence of a fairly active membership is

Table 6.4. Membership of other voluntary organizations (%)

Type of organization/group	Now	In past
Trade union	18.5	37.9
Church or religious group	22.5	19.5
School board/PTA	3.3	16.2
Elderly or disabled group	7.5	10.3
Arts, music or cultural group	15.9	13.4
Local community action group	7.8	11.5
Third world development organization	7.2	5.4
Conservation group	18.1	10.9
Professional association	20.9	17.6
Youth work	5.2	24.2
Sports club or recreation group	16.4	17.9
Women's group	3.7	6.8
Peace movement group	4.5	8.8
Human rights group	6.2	6.2
Environmental group	6.9	6.0
Other political party	–	13.5

confirmed when we examine its role in the community (Table 6.4). As we saw in Chapter 5, as well as membership of trade unions/professional association, churches, and arts and sports groups, participation in conservation groups, youth groups, school boards, and local community action groups is prominent. Nearly a third has been involved in a youth group, suggesting high levels of contributions to local communities. These findings suggest that the kind of people who join the SNP tend to belong to multiple associations and groups; that is, they are 'joiners' who participate in many different ways. This includes having been members of other parties prior to joining the SNP. Nearly one in seven (13.5 per cent) of the respondents had been members of other political parties: of these, 44 per cent were formerly in the Labour Party; 20 per cent in the Conservative Party; 12 per cent in the Liberals or Liberal Democrats; 4 per cent in the Scottish Socialist Party or Solidarity; 3 per cent in the Greens; 3 per cent in Plaid Cymru, the SNP's sister party in Wales; and 15 per cent in other parties (including those outside the United Kingdom ranging from the German Social Democrats to the Canadian New Democratic Party).

Parties have recently harnessed the Internet (Bruter and Harrison, 2009a, 2009b), as a campaigning tool for targeting supporters, for communicating with members or for encouraging web participation (Gibson and Ward, 2000; Oates et al., 2006). Web-based interaction between parties and members has the potential to transform internal democracy, perhaps leading to a new type of member who is not active in a traditional sense by attending meetings but is contributing to internal debate and decision-making via a party website. Margetts (2010: 78) suggests a 'new ideal type of political party, the "cyber party"'. A majority of SNP members had accessed the party's headquarters website in the previous year but only a minority had done so frequently: 7 per cent had done so at least once a week; 20 per cent around once a month; 34 per cent not as often as that; and 39 per cent had not done so, the last figure including those with no access to the Web. Less than a third had accessed the members-only-section on the party's website.

So far, we have been examining levels and forms of participation in the SNP. However, this says nothing about the relationship between different types of activism. Through factor analysis of the correlations between the various forms of activity, it can be seen whether and how different forms of party activity cluster together, whether groups of members participate in particular ways. A factor analysis of those items contained in Table 6.3 produces a one-dimensional outcome. There is little evidence that members specialize in certain *types* of activity. Instead, what distinguishes members is the *amount* of activity.

However, when we expand the factor analysis to include measures of financial donations and other measures of seniority – office-bearing responsibilities and standing as a candidate – a different pattern emerges suggesting the existence of quite distinct forms of activism. Table 6.5

Table 6.5. Factor analysis of activism

	Factor 1 – activity	Factor 2 – office	Factor 3 – financial
How active in the party	0.841	0.115	−0.191
How often attend local meetings	0.772	0.033	−0.170
Hours devoted to party per month	0.690	0.071	0.246
Money to local party	0.365	0.054	0.400
Money to national party	0.196	0.103	0.758
Displayed an election poster	0.653	0.027	0.179
Attended national conference	0.618	−0.198	−0.097
Delivered election leaflets	0.864	−0.012	0.111
Delivered leaflets between elections	0.862	−0.020	0.083
Helped at a party function	0.819	−0.068	0.026
Canvassed door-to-door	0.751	−0.169	0.039
Canvassed by telephone	0.494	−0.255	−0.027
Ever been candidate for SNP	0.053	0.774	0.016
Branch office-bearer	−0.106	0.756	0.003
Constituency office-bearer	0.058	0.866	0.026
How often access website	0.167	0.047	0.620

displays the results from this analysis of SNP activism.[2] Factor 1 is a traditional 'activity' factor, with the key general measures of time and meetings, and the various election-work indicators. The only questions loading on the second factor are 'office' items. Factor 3 represents the financial (and, more weakly, the website) side of party involvement. This third factor is distinct from the other two, correlating at less than 0.25 with each of them. This weak correlation between the financial factor and the other two factors supports our earlier contention, based on Figure 6.1, that there are substantial numbers of SNP members who contribute large amounts of money but do not do much else in the party and that there are many members who are quite active but do not pay much to the party. The correlation between activity and office-holding is stronger which suggests that those who do one tend to do more of the other. In other words, those who hold office are likely to be unusually active within the party but there are, of course, some members who are very active but have neither sought nor held office.

The results contain the message that making financial donations and, to some extent holding office in the party are different from other forms of activity, such as attending meetings and helping out at elections. Of further note is the fact that election activities load on the same factor as attending internal party meetings; that is, these tasks do not represent different dimensions of activism, a finding that differs from some other studies of party activists. Cross and Young (2008: 262) differentiate between 'campaign activism' and 'intra-party democracy'. The discrete categories of activism in the SNP appear to be: traditional grass roots activities, which *include* campaigning; holding office in the party; and making financial contributions. Making financial donations to the party for some members might be viewed as a form of surrogate participation.

These findings are similar to those in studies of pressure group supporters. Large numbers of pressure group supporters will never seek to become involved in the internal decision-making of groups but provide important financial support (Jordan and Maloney, 1997, 2007; Maloney, 2009). In parties such as the SNP, there are more meaningful opportunities for members to become involved than in pressure groups as parties tend to be more democratic. However, a section of the SNP membership prefers to remain passive and to contribute funds rather than time.

---

[2] An item is deemed to belong to a factor if its loading is 0.4 or above.

Who are the activists?

Previous studies of parties and their members have explored the relationship between social characteristics and participation, with a view to identifying those factors that facilitate or encourage activism. Here we do the same for the SNP, using the activism index outlined above as our measure of activity. As Table 6.6 shows, SNP activists are disproportionately male, in common with the membership as a whole and typical of other party studies. SNP activists are relatively middle-aged, confirming trends apparent in international data that younger generations are less inclined to participate in political parties (Morales, 2009; Whiteley, 2009). Some studies of civic voluntarism and civic engagement have explored the possibility that political activism is related to having spare time, for example, due to being retired (Whiteley, 2009). However, the SNP data suggest that those who are self-employed or in full-time employment are most likely to be active and retired members least active. Graduates, the relatively well off and those with middle-class identities all tend towards higher levels of activity. Finally, it comes as no surprise that those respondents with young children look considerably less likely to be active.

Regression analysis allows us to explore the forces behind activism in greater detail and, in particular, to identify those characteristics and attitudes that are associated with greater activism even holding the other forces or factors constant. The analysis presented in Table 6.7 explores the correlates of activism among SNP members, and because we have been able to identify distinct aspects of activism, we can test regression models on the three types distinguished in the factor analysis in Table 6.5. The regression results are presented in Table 6.7.

When other drivers are held constant, occupational class is not significantly related to patterns of activism, except in the case of financial contributions. As might be expected, there is a tendency for those in professional and managerial occupations, and with higher incomes, to contribute more funds to the party. Higher incomes allow members to donate more but income is not a particularly important determinant of the other dimensions of activity. That said, those on higher incomes are not any *less* active in other ways, challenging any suggestion that supporting the party financially *compensates* for being inactive in other ways. There is also a positive relationship between education, especially having a degree, and making a financial contribution. The influence of education also applies to office-holding within the party.

Table 6.6. Activism and social characteristics (%)

	Very inactive	Occasionally active	Fairly active	Very active
All	7.7	51.8	36.5	4.0
N	*546*	*3679*	*2592*	*282*
Sex				
Female	7.8	53.9	34.4	3.9
Male	4.0	53.0	38.9	4.2
Age (year)				
18–34	3.6	55.8	37.3	3.2
35–44	4.0	59.8	33.4	3.1
45–54	4.0	55.4	35.9	4.7
55–64	4.9	50.6	38.9	5.5
65–74	5.1	49.9	41.4	3.6
75+	8.1	55.3	33.5	3.1
Occupational class				
Professional/higher managerial	4.7	52.1	38.2	5.0
Intermediate/clerical/skilled manual/ lower managerial	4.7	55.8	36.5	3.1
Routine/semi-routine manual/service	6.3	53.7	37.6	2.4
Employment status				
Employed full-time	3.6	53.4	38.2	4.9
Employed part-time	4.9	53.3	38.1	3.7
Self-employed	3.6	53.7	37.4	5.2
Retired	6.0	52.9	37.5	3.6
Income				
Under £10,000	7.2	56.1	35.2	1.5
£10,000–30,000	4.7	51.8	39.8	3.6
£30,000–50,000	2.8	51.9	40.3	5.1
£50,000+	3.7	53.7	35.9	6.6
Children				
0–5	3.3	63.0	31.3	2.4
5–15	3.5	56.3	36.9	3.2
Highest qualification				
None	7.1	57.2	33.1	2.6
Standard/'O' Level/GCSE	5.2	55.5	35.8	3.5
Higher/ 'A' Level/vocational	5.0	51.9	38.9	4.2
Degree	4.2	52.4	38.3	5.1
Urban/rural				
City	4.9	55.6	35.6	3.9
Suburbs of city	6.8	58.5	31.6	3.1
Small town	5.1	51.2	38.9	4.8
Village/country	4.6	51.9	39.5	4.0

The basic bivariate relationship indicates that women are less active than men (Table 6.6). However, Table 6.7 suggests that traditional forms of activity are *not* significantly related to sex; that is, women are not less likely to be involved in internal party activities. It is when it comes to holding office and making financial contributions, that women are less

Table 6.7. Determinants of activism (regression of different activism scales)

	Activity		Office		Finance	
	Beta	Sig.	Beta	Sig.	Beta	Sig.
Sex (female)	0.017	0.203	−0.025	0.049	−0.133	0.000
Age	−0.097	0.000	−0.010	0.666	−0.099	0.000
Age squared	−0.047	0.004	−0.087	0.000	0.005	0.764
Occupational Class (routine manual/service)						
Professional/higher managerial	−0.040	0.065	−0.010	0.623	0.089	0.000
Intermed/skilled manual/ lower managerial	−0.008	0.690	0.030	0.102	0.067	0.001
Employment status (other/ not specified)						
Employed full-time/self-employed	−0.026	0.132	0.006	0.723	0.004	0.837
Employed part-time	0.012	0.394	−0.012	0.371	−0.002	0.901
Retired	0.000	0.988	−0.029	0.135	−0.009	0.680
Income (not specified)						
<£10,000	−0.012	0.431	−0.017	0.245	−0.028	0.088
£10,000–30,000	0.023	0.207	−0.004	0.824	0.079	0.000
£30,000–50,000	0.000	0.984	0.009	0.593	0.081	0.000
>£50,000	−0.024	0.180	0.002	0.888	0.159	0.000
Educational qualifications (up to 15/16 only)						
Some post-16	0.003	0.855	0.050	0.002	0.038	0.033
Degree	−0.017	0.386	0.037	0.050	0.050	0.019
Children (none)						
Under 5	−0.032	0.018	0.001	0.951	−0.039	0.006
Between 5 and 15	−0.009	0.500	0.008	0.538	−0.031	0.032
Urban/rural (rural area)						
City	−0.040	0.009	−0.005	0.736	0.012	0.434
Suburb	−0.062	0.000	−0.020	0.146	0.008	0.590
Small town	−0.019	0.217	0.022	0.138	−0.002	0.913
Year first joined	−0.334	0.000	−0.523	0.000	−0.023	0.240
Year first joined squared	−0.156	0.000	−0.148	0.000	0.006	0.688
Why joined						
For independence/anti-union	−0.037	0.144	−0.057	0.012	0.029	0.243
Defend/support Scotland	−0.015	0.400	−0.043	0.013	0.023	0.219
Other issue/ideology	−0.001	0.928	−0.007	0.638	0.030	0.072
Liked party/leader	−0.035	0.051	−0.033	0.060	0.029	0.122
Disliked other party	−0.035	0.026	−0.015	0.337	0.021	0.197
Actively asked	0.018	0.295	−0.011	0.511	0.029	0.102
To participate	−0.047	0.002	−0.036	0.016	0.002	0.904
Membership lapsed since first joined	−0.133	0.000	−.143	0.000	−0.021	0.167
Number of other groups participated in	0.077	0.000	0.006	0.653	0.056	0.000
Never member of other party	−0.004	0.745	0.002	0.898	0.016	0.255
Internal efficacy	0.281	0.000	0.262	0.000	0.142	0.000

(continued)

Table 6.7. Continued

	Activity		Office		Finance	
	Beta	Sig.	Beta	Sig.	Beta	Sig.
External efficacy outside party	0.194	0.000	0.021	0.135	0.050	0.001
External efficacy within party	−0.028	0.046	−0.029	0.030	0.058	0.000
Evaluation of Salmond	−0.025	0.072	−0.062	0.000	0.003	0.860
More pragmatic (six-item scale)	−0.042	0.003	−0.041	0.002	−0.012	0.425
Constitutional preference (independence in EU)						
Favour more powers	−0.019	0.163	−0.019	0.140	−0.052	0.000
Independence outside EU	−0.028	0.034	−0.028	0.032	−0.032	0.025
Towards 'British' end of scale	−0.046	0.001	−0.039	0.003	−0.044	0.002
More right-wing (six-item scale)	0.016	0.235	0.037	0.005	0.046	0.002
More authoritarian (six-item scale)	−0.087	0.000	−0.130	0.000	−0.108	0.000

involved. This is explained by a tendency for women to be active in specific ways – being prepared to organize local level party functions and fundraising events rather than taking on formal decision-making positions.

This brings us to the impact of family commitments on political participation, an under-explored theme in the literature. The bivariate relationship points to lower average rates of activism amongst members, both women and men, with very young children. The regression analysis indicates that the existence of children influences traditional forms of activism as well as financial commitments. In the former case, having children under 5 reduces the likelihood of involvement and having any children decreases financial donations. These findings provide evidence that the time and financial commitments associated with having children suppress participation. However, the effect is not strong and it is notable how little activity seems to be inhibited by having children. Given that women are usually the main child carers, we would expect constraints on activity amongst women with children to be greater than amongst men with children. There is some evidence that younger children inhibit mothers' activities more than fathers', although it is hard to judge given that the SNP has few women with younger children. It may be that young families act more as a barrier to joining the party than to being active within it. In that case, those members who clear that barrier are already unusual, and perhaps more likely to be active than might otherwise be expected and may well have had children since joining.

There is a strong relationship between the time of joining and levels of activism, as we might expect as it can take time to learn the ways of activism. The newest recruits are particularly inactive. That said, many of the party's senior members interviewed for this study remarked on the speed with which they became active members. Those who joined in the 1970s are more active than those who joined in the 1990s. The relationship between reasons for joining and activity is complex. Those motivated by independence or a desire to promote Scottish interests are less likely to hold office in the party and those who were motivated to join the SNP because they disliked another party are less likely to be active. Ironically, those who say they joined to participate are *less* likely to be active. An explanation may lie in perceptions of what it means to be active. Unlike in pressure groups, becoming a member of a party is more likely to be considered a political act in and of itself, regardless of whether a member becomes otherwise active. Finally, those who have allowed their membership to lapse at some point tend to be less active and being a member of another group slightly enhances the chances of being active in the party.

Activism and radicalism

Theoretical accounts of parties lead to expectations that activists will have inflexible, ideological opinions relative to passive members and party leaders (May, 1973; Kitschelt, 1994). According to this perspective, activists can inconvenience party leaders by supporting ideas and strategies that are unpalatable to voters, while leaders and passive members are seen to be more moderate, pragmatic, and in-tune with voter opinion. Some have suggested that the professionalization of parties has involved leaders attempting to by-pass activists by giving more power to ordinary members in candidate selection, leadership elections, and policy development (Mair, 1994; Scarrow et al., 2000; Webb, 2000). Research on groups also suggests that having 'supporters' rather than active members 'circumvents the problems of internal democracy and policy interference' (Maloney, 2009: 279).

As we argued in Chapter 3, the SNP has increasingly demonstrated many of the characteristics of a professional party. However, the evidence presented in this chapter suggests that this is compatible with a relatively vibrant active membership. To examine activism and attitudes in the SNP, we now look at some more measures of opinion and compare the various forms of activism, including a number of 'sub-groups', such

Table 6.8. Activism, national identity, and constitutional preferences (%)

	Scottish only	Some British	Independence in EU	Independence out of EU	More powers
Very inactive	72	28	62	22	15
2	77	24	64	21	15
3	80	20	66	24	11
4	83	17	65	24	11
Very active	89	11	73	19	8
Conference regular	88	12	73	19	8
Local meeting regular	81	19	64	24	11
Election worker	85	15	69	21	10
Office none	76	24	63	23	14
Branch/constituency office	85	15	67	23	10
Unsuccessful candidate	88	12	73	21	6
Councillor	92	8	77	17	5
National position	89	11	77	17	6
Finance lowest	77	23	57	26	18
2	78	22	67	21	12
3	80	20	66	23	11
4	81	19	74	20	6
Finance highest	87	14	79	17	4
Total/all members	*80*	*20*	*66*	*22*	*12*

as election workers, those who attend conferences on a regular basis, and councillors compared with the membership as a whole.

Table 6.8 contains data on national identity and constitutional preferences. The association between an exclusive Scottish identity and activism is quite striking. As a general rule, more active respondents feel more Scottish and less British than the membership as a whole. This applies to all measures of activism, with the passive members looking least 'Scottish' and SNP councillors the most 'Scottish' of all: only 8 per cent of councillors describe themselves as at all British, compared to one in four of very inactive members.

The data on attitudes towards the constitution suggest that the most active tend to be the most supportive of independence in the European Union (EU). Conference attendees, for example, are a little more supportive of independence in Europe than those who do not attend regularly; and office-holders are considerably more likely to support the policy than non-office holding or passive members. This tendency is most pronounced for financial activism. Four-fifths of those who contribute most support this constitutional option compared to just over half of those who contribute least. The evidence suggests that activity is related to a commitment to independence in Europe. The least active are more likely to opt for 'more powers' as their first choice and they are also a little more likely to prefer independence outside the EU. The picture is one of consensus around the party's constitutional objective with the passive members most likely to take a slightly different position. Overall, the passive members are more varied in their responses, both in terms of their national identity and constitutional objectives, while activists of all types are more united. That said, insofar as the SNP's current policy is more sympathetic to a gradualist approach to independence, via further devolution, these passive members should not be characterized as at odds with the party.

The link between activism and support for independence is reinforced by the structure of opinions on the strategic direction of the party. The more active respondents are more likely to agree that the pursuit of independence should be the priority and all else secondary. Councillors take the most uncompromising stance: 81 per cent of councillors but only 67 per cent of non-office-holders agree that independence should be the SNP's primary goal and all else should be secondary.

Activists in the party are also more likely to disagree with the suggestion that the goal of independence may need to take second place. The differences between the least and most active are pronounced: 72 per cent of the very inactive but only 56 per cent of the most active agree with the statement. Meanwhile the office-holders in a national position look the least flexible on this item: 46 per cent agree, compared with 69 per cent of non-office-holders.

In Chapter 8 we show that SNP members view themselves as slightly left of centre. The most active members are considerably more likely to describe themselves as left-wing: 58 per cent of the very active identify as such compared with 46 per cent of the passive members; very inactive members are also likely to see themselves as left-wing but a higher proportion regard themselves as right-wing than do active members. The relationship between activism and left-wing identity is most clear for the office-holders. Councillors and those holding a national office appear the most left-wing of all. However, making a financial contribution is rather different: the more 'financially active' are not much more likely to identify as left-wing and are equally likely to regard themselves as right-wing as the least financially active (Table 6.9). One obvious explanation is that those members who can afford to make substantial donations are less than enthusiastic about left-wing economic policies.

According to May's law (May, 1973), activists are held to be the most radical group in a party, that is, the expectation is of a direct relationship

Table 6.9. Activism and left–right self-placement (%)

	Left	Centre	Right
Very inactive	46	25	30
2	46	27	27
3	48	27	25
4	47	26	27
Very active	58	22	21
Conference regular	56	23	22
Local meeting regular	56	21	23
Election worker	52	22	26
Office none	46	27	28
Branch/constituency office	53	24	23
Unsuccessful candidate	54	23	23
Councillor	60	21	19
National position	61	17	22
Finance lowest	48	27	26
2	48	27	26
3	49	25	25
4	53	23	25
Finance highest	52	23	26
Total/all members	*48*	*24*	*28*

between activism and radicalism. In the SNP, the link between activism and radicalism is more complex. Activists tend to be more hard line on independence, on the party's strategic direction, and in their ideological identities than inactive members but the extent of this radical activism should not be exaggerated. The membership as a whole is remarkably pragmatic. However, where as May's law leads us to expect to see curvi-linearity, that is, more moderate views amongst those closest to power, the evidence here is more mixed. Office-holders in the SNP appear most radical in some respects and the councillors are distinctly 'Scottish' and reluctant to cooperate with other parties. However, elite interviews confirm the pragmatism of the party's leadership at national level, providing more supportive evidence of May's law. Pragmatic acceptance of party strategy was evident in these interviews even amongst senior members previously regarded as hardliners.

Conclusion

Activism in a party is more complex than is often assumed. In the SNP, there are three prominent dimensions of activism: traditional; office-holding; and financial. While there is some overlap between the first two, that is, many activists perform both roles, financial participation looks most distinct. This confirms the existence of a largely passive armchair supporter element willing to contribute funds or set up a bank order but unwilling or unable to give time and energy to other party activities. The SNP membership data suggest that the very idea of 'financial activism' may be a misnomer. There is a body of members who make financial contributions but little else. These members stand out, at least in degree, from those who conform to a more orthodox understanding of political activism. However, the evidence also suggests that the SNP maintains vibrant grass roots, with activists sustaining the party's organizational structure and election campaigns. The SNP appears to have combined modern and traditional party forms of activity successfully.

Despite evidence of a link between activism and radical views, the active members appear content with the strategic direction of the party, and with the internal distribution of power. Members show remarkable levels of support for the leadership. Part of the reason for this, no doubt, was that the survey was conducted shortly after the SNP became Scotland's largest party for the first time. There is little sign of a 'troublesome layer' of activists set on challenging the party leadership (Mair, 1994: 16).

However, in common with other parties, the SNP is plagued by an inability to encourage a broad range of social types to become active. The lack of women and young members among the activist base should be an obvious concern for the party. Indeed, while the party's membership has been increasing in recent years it is still well short of the figures, even accounting for exaggerated estimates, of the past. It may be that modern campaigning techniques are replacing traditional doorstep campaigning but activists in a party such as the SNP, with very little media support, cannot entirely do without its members in campaigning. However, modern techniques may be allowing its older members, the foot soldiers of past campaigns, to continue active campaigning.

7

Nations, National Identity, and Nationalism

Introduction

In this chapter, we explore members' views of the Scottish nation and national identity. Nations have been defined as 'imagined communities' (Anderson, 1983). A nation is imagined in the sense that its members cannot know others in the national community though 'in the minds of each lives the image of their communion' (Ibid.: 15). Smith argues that one feature of the imagined community is that it is conceived as a 'deep, horizontal comradeship' (Smith, 1991: 16). Bechhofer and McCrone have argued that 'national identity' is the 'poor relation' of the trilogy that also includes 'nation' and 'nationalism' and too often seen as derivative of the other concepts (Bechhofer and McCrone, 2010: 18; see also Norman, 2006: 33). Smith has defined national identity as involving 'some sort of political community, however tenuous... It also suggests a definite social space, a fairly well demarcated and bounded territory, with which the members identify and to which they feel they belong' (Smith, 1991: 9). For Bechhofer and McCrone, national identity is the 'political–cultural identification with territory' (McCrone and Bechhofer, 2008: 1245). Following Goffman (1959, 1961), they see identities as negotiated in the sense that people reach agreements on 'who is who'. Individuals will choose 'identity markers' defined as 'characteristics associated with an individual that they might choose to present to others, in order to support a national identity claim' (Kiely et al., 2001: 35–6).

Primary and secondary identities

Before considering the nature of Scottish identity among our respondents, we begin by examining its salience relative to other identities. As expected of the Scottish National Party (SNP), national identity is overwhelmingly dominant among primary identities, and was ranked first or second by more than four out of five members (Table 7.1) in response to a question asking respondents to list how they think of or describe themselves in order of importance. However, it may be striking that only 65 per cent of SNP members gave national identity as their first ranked identity with the remaining split fairly evenly across a range of other identities. Scottish identity appears to be a unifying factor but perhaps less so than we might expect. As we will see in the next chapter, support for independence is a more important unifying factor for SNP members than Scottish identity. Place of residence and political allegiance were the most favoured secondary identities amongst those who saw national identity as their primary identity, although each accounts for only around one in five responses. The reluctance to acknowledge a class identity is also evident. Gender is cited by relatively few respondents, mainly women. It tended to be younger and older women members who mentioned gender as a primary or secondary identity.

The standard measurement of Scottish national identity in social science research gauges the *direction* rather than the *strength* of national identity. This measure asks respondents to locate themselves on a five-point scale running from 'Scottish not British' to 'British not Scottish'. In Table 7.2, we show how SNP members and, for comparison, SNP voters and the electorate as a whole in 2007 split between the five options. The party's members were highly likely – in both absolute and relative terms – to identify themselves as exclusively Scottish.

Table 7.1. Primary and secondary identities among SNP members (%)

	First ranked	Second ranked
National identity	65	16
Job	7	14
Age group/generation	6	15
Gender	6	8
Religion	5	6
Place where you live	4	16
Social class	2	6
Political allegiance	2	15
Ethnicity	1	3
Other	3	1
N	*6538*	*6459*

Table 7.2. Scottish-to-British national identity among SNP members, SNP voters, and the electorate (%)

	SNP members	SNP voters	Electorate
Scottish not British	80	43	28
More Scottish than British	17	39	32
Equally Scottish and British	3	15	29
More British than Scottish	0	2	5
British not Scottish	0	1	6
N	*6537*	*277*	*1414*

For the purposes of clean comparison, we exclude those giving 'Other' responses.

While SNP voters clearly feel less British than the average Scot, it is party members that form the really distinct group: 80 per cent of members choose the 'Scottish not British' option with only a tiny fraction reporting a primary British identity. Significantly, however, 20 per cent acknowledge some British identity. This same proportion emerged in response to different questions: 21 per cent agreed that 'Sometimes it is more appropriate to say you are British and sometimes it is more appropriate to say you are Scottish' and 19 per cent agreed that 'You can be equally proud of being British and of being Scottish; it's not a matter of choosing between them.' It is striking that, in interviews with senior members of the party, very few were willing to acknowledge any British component to their identity and then only when prompted. The almost universal view of these senior figures was a rejection of Britishness in any shape or form.

As noted earlier, these attachments can vary in a number of ways. One such is the extent to which they are felt emotionally. Two survey questions addressed this point. The first simply asked respondents to say how proud, if at all, they felt of being Scottish. An overwhelming majority of respondents felt either 'very proud' (83 per cent) or 'fairly proud' (15 per cent). A rather stiffer test of emotional identification comes with the statement 'When someone criticizes Scotland, it feels like a personal insult.' Overall, 70 per cent of respondents agreed with this statement, split fairly evenly between 'strongly agree' and 'agree', while 15 per cent disagreed and only 3 per cent 'strongly' disagreed.

Turning now to the issue of what members are identifying *with* when they report Scottish identity, we begin with responses to the following question: 'Being Scottish has lots of different aspects, some of which are listed below. Which, if any, of these is important to you personally when you think about being Scottish?' This was another ranking question and in Table 7.3 we report respondents' first two choices. The most popular choice was the 'people'. The Scottish Parliament and democratic

Table 7.3. Aspects of being Scottish personally important to members (%)

	First ranked	Second ranked
People	44	17
History	13	20
Scottish Parliament	12	12
Countryside/scenery	11	15
Democratic tradition	10	11
Education/science	4	11
Art/music/literature	3	7
Legal system	2	4
Sporting achievements	1	2
Other	1	0
N	*6505*	*6478*

tradition together suggest a notable degree of satisfaction with institutions and traditions that have been the focus of critical attention by the party. It might have been expected that fewer SNP members would have ranked the devolved Scottish Parliament highly, given that it operates within constraints that the party aims to remove. Those identifying the 'democratic tradition' may have been identifying a Scottish ideal, such as that associated with the 'democratic intellect', rather than expressing confidence in existing institutions.

Who is the 'other'?

A common implicit theme in writing on national identity is the importance of the 'outgroup' or 'other' (Triandafyllidou, 1988). Individuals identifying with a nation do so in large part by distinguishing themselves from some 'other' or 'others'. These 'others' are seen not only as alternative identities but also as potential or real threats. Members were asked to rank the three most important threats over the years to the Scottish nation (Table 7.4). The two most cited reasons have less to do with identifying some external threat than internal concerns: being denied access to North Sea oil revenues; and a lack of self-confidence. English nationalism and immigration from England hardly register and are the two least cited threats by party members. London Government was mentioned amongst the top three threats by about half of respondents and the perceived threat posed by Thatcherism, which might be interpreted as a subset of London Government, is identified as one of the top three threats by a quarter of members.

There are differences in perceived threats by age and period of joining the party. 'London Government' is seen as a much bigger threat by

Table 7.4. Threats to Scottish nation (%)

Threats	First ranked	Second ranked	None
Being denied North Sea oil revenues	23.9	20.5	41.3
Lack of self-confidence as a nation	23.3	10.7	55.0
London Government	17.2	16.3	51.0
Thatcherism	11.0	7.1	75.3
Nuclear weapons	6.4	10.0	75.0
Nuclear waste	2.8	5.0	85.5
Foreign ownership of Scottish businesses	2.6	5.2	84.4
Immigration from outside the UK	2.4	2.9	92.0
Emigration	2.3	4.1	88.8
Immigration from England	2.0	2.5	92.6
European Union policies	1.9	3.6	91.0
Mass media	1.7	4.8	86.4
English nationalism	0.6	1.0	96.7

younger than older members though there are no significant differences by when members joined the party. The contingency coefficient for the differences by cohort is slightly higher (0.18) than the corresponding coefficient for the differences by age (0.14). So perceived threats vary slightly more by when respondents joined the party than by when they were born. Nonetheless, both have a significant (and different) relationship with perceived threat. There are differences in terms of 'lack of self-confidence' with this threat becoming a progressively more troublesome aspect to members the longer they have been in the party. This may reflect socialization as 'lack of self-confidence' was commented upon by many senior members interviewed. At first sight, the findings on 'Thatcherism' seem unusual. There is little variation, according to when members joined the party, amongst those who saw 'Thatcherism' as a threat. It might have been expected that those who joined between 1980 and 1988 would be most likely to mention 'Thatcherism' when in fact a slightly higher proportion of those who joined after 2001 saw 'Thatcherism' as a threat. In part, this may come down to understandings of 'Thatcherism', with some members viewing New Labour as continuing to adopt 'Thatcherite' policies or may simply reflect Mrs Thatcher's lingering impact on Scottish politics.

Civic and ethnic identities

One of the most enduring distinctions in the study of national identity has been that between ethnic and civic national identities. Binary distinctions of this kind have had a long-standing appeal to students of nations and nationalism dating back to Friedrich Meinecke, who argued at the beginning of the twentieth century that a sharp distinction existed between political and cultural nationalism (Meinecke [1907] 1970). This distinction is unhelpful in understanding modern Scottish politics given the breadth of identification with the Scottish nation. Donald Dewar, the first Labour First Minister of Scotland, described himself as a 'cultural nationalist' (Gray, 2002: 7). Indeed, by the end of the twentieth century, political parties operating in Scotland that failed to emphasize their Scottish credentials could expect to suffer electorally. Binary distinctions can be unhelpful in understanding nations (Nieguth, 1999).

The origins of the ethnic–civic distinction lie in historical analyses of nationalism. The work of Hans Kohn (especially Kohn, 1944) in particular has been influential. Kohn traced the history of the idea of nationalism in Europe. The underlying theme of his work was the relationship between nationalism and liberalism (Calhoun, 2007: ch. 6). Western nationalism, Kohn maintained, was essentially political, voluntarist, and had been influenced by Enlightenment ideas. In 'backward' Eastern Europe, the nation is organic. It precedes and aims to create the state unlike in Western Europe where the state precedes the nation (see Kuzio (2002) for a critique of Kohn's distinction). Others who have either adopted this terminology or equivalent have had similar normative motives – that is, distinguishing between 'good' and 'bad' nationalisms. In parallel with Kohn's civic (American) and ethnic (German) nationalism in the inter-war and early post-war period, Plamenatz distinguished between Eastern (bad) and Western (good) nationalism (Plamenatz, 1973). Brubacker used the ethnic–civic distinction in his comparative study of French and German nationalisms (Brubaker, 1992), arguing that this was relevant to the different ways in which these two states were formed. In recent times, authors such as William Pfaff (1993) and Michael Ignatieff (1994) have used the dichotomy as the basis for polemics against particular nationalisms.

This theoretical literature is largely based on historical analysis or concerned with political philosophical concerns. There is little that explores nationalist movements but rather the focus is on (perceptions of) nations or even states. The dichotomy is rarely tested empirically in the literature. McCrone has asked:

> While the analytical value of the civic/ethnic distinction has been put to good use ... it does lend itself to ethnocentric caricature – why can't *they* be more like *us*? It is also a distinction which can be criticised on analytical

grounds. Is it, for example, possible to maintain such a distinction in practice? How is one to make sense of endemic racism against 'Other' in Western societies which profess overwhelmingly civic definitions of citizens? Further, Chateaubriand's comment about people being willing to die for passions but not for interests is apposite here. How in practice can these be kept apart? Are 'blood' and 'soil' so distinct, and does not the latter imply the former? (McCrone, 1988: 9)

Yack has raised similar concerns:

the civic/ethnic dichotomy parallels a series of contrasts that should set off alarm bells: not only Western/Eastern, but rational/emotive, voluntary/ inherited, good/bad, ours/theirs! Designed to protect us from the dangers of ethnocentric politics, the civic/ethnic distinction itself reflects a considerable dose of ethnocentrism, as if the political identities *French* and *American* were not also culturally inherited artifacts, no matter how much they develop and change as they pass from generation to generation. The characterization of political community in the so-called civic nations as a rational and freely chosen allegiance to a set of political principles seems untenable to me, a mixture of self-congratulations and wishful thinking. (Yack, 1999: 105)

In a study comparing the ethnic and civic distinction across Europe, Schulman (2002) focused on attitudes of members of various 'nations' (in fact states). After analysing public opinion data from fifteen states, Schulman concluded that the dichotomy is a 'gross simplification of concepts of nationhood in the West, Central Europe, and Eastern Europe' (Ibid.: 582–3). In addition to making an important empirical contribution, Schulman identified a number of conceptual problems with the distinction. In its place, he proposed that the 'three main variants for the content of national identity are *civic*, *cultural*, and *ethnic*' (Schulman, 2002: 559) (Figure 7.1).

Content of National Identity	Key Components
Civic	Territory Citizenship Will and consent Political ideology Political institutions and rights
Cultural	Religion Language Traditions
Ethnic	Ancestry Race

Figure 7.1. Alternative contents of national identity
Source: Schulman (2002: 559).

The civic–ethnic distinction has entered political discourse in Scotland and, while this may not have had an impact on the public at large, SNP politicians are quick to describe themselves as civic nationalists. It should be stressed that conceptions of identity are not the same as conceptions of citizenship, though these are often conflated. Citizenship concerns the relationship between the individual and the state: rights; duties; and responsibilities. It also involves membership and a state can define membership, as citizenship, either relatively inclusively or exclusively. Though conceptually distinct, we would expect the definition of national identity to be closely related to notions of citizenship. SNP policy is a model of civic citizenship initially drawn up in a draft constitution for an independent Scotland in 1977, chiefly drafted by legal theorist and SNP Vice President Neil MacCormick (MacCormick, 2000: 721). MacCormick later described the key provision:

> Who shall be citizens? – All persons principally resident in Scotland and all those who were born in Scotland, with no restriction on dual citizenship; a free right to renounce citizenship, with no less of residential rights in the case of renounced citizenship; absolute prohibition on any loss of citizenship otherwise than by fully voluntary renunciation.   (MacCormick, 1999, 2000)

One commentator on the draft constitution, as revised in 2002, has remarked that it was remarkable in being

> devoid of nationalism. There is no preamble, no stirring words about 'national struggle', no ringing declaration of liberty equality and fraternity. It does not even specify a flag or an anthem. This is a functional document, a basic framework of democracy, not an ideological statement. (Bulmer, 2011, forthcoming)

The SNP's draft constitution for an independent Scotland states SNP support for 'an inclusive Scotland that embraces its geographic and cultural diversity, where its citizens are free from discrimination on any grounds in the exercise of their constitutional rights' (SNP, 2002: 7). It can therefore be assumed that, amongst SNP activists, the idea that the SNP is a civic nationalist party will be familiar both in the use of the term but, more importantly, in terms of policies on multiculturalism, immigration, and citizenship, and most academic discussions of the party have categorized it as civic in nationalist outlook (Keating, 1996; Lynch, 2002).

Amongst the many statements setting out the party's civic credentials in its definition of citizenship was a speech delivered by Alex Salmond in October 2007 in New York, in which he argued for a 'peaceful, inclusive, civic nationalism – one born of tolerance and respect for all faiths, colours and creeds and one which will continue to inspire constitutional evolution based on a positive vision of what our nation can be' (Salmond, 2007). The SNP takes pride that one of its members, Bashir Ahmad, became the first Asian Member of the Scottish Parliament in 2007. His speech at the SNP's 1995 conference, in which he argued that 'it isn't important where you come from, what matters is where we are going together as a nation', received a standing ovation and was quoted by a number of senior party members in interviews for this study (*Independent*, 14 February 2009). Further emphasizing its liberal credentials, the party campaigns for a more liberal policy on asylum seekers and immigration.

Who are the 'people'?

The dominant response in Table 7.3, the 'people', raises the distinction between ethnic and civic national identities. Does the 'people' refer to an ethnic group with a common ancestry or to the voluntary members of a political community? In order to address this issue and to test the characterization of the SNP as a civic nationalist party, we asked members about the importance of various characteristics for a person to be considered 'truly Scottish'. Responses are reported in Table 7.5, along with a calculation of the mean importance of each characteristic based on coding the scale from 0 (not at all important) to 3 (very important).

Broadly speaking, these results vindicate those who have characterized the SNP as a party with a civic conception of national identity. Hardly any respondents dismissed 'feeling Scottish' and 'respecting Scottish political institutions' as unimportant. Living in Scotland was

Table 7.5. Importance of characteristics for being 'truly Scottish' (%)

How important is ___ to be truly Scottish?	Very	Fairly	Not very	Not at all	Mean (0–3)
To have Scottish ancestry	24	32	27	17	1.6
To have been born in Scotland	33	30	22	15	1.8
To live in Scotland now	48	32	15	6	2.2
To have lived in Scotland for most of one's life	28	37	26	9	1.8
To be a Christian	12	13	19	56	0.8
To respect Scottish political institutions and laws	59	34	5	2	2.5
To feel Scottish	78	18	3	1	2.7
To be able to speak English, Gaelic, or Scots	39	34	17	10	2.0

seen as considerably more important than having been born in Scotland. The two most obviously ethnic characteristics – having Scottish
ancestry and being born in Scotland – are also quite widely regarded as
relevant for national identity, both described as 'very' or 'fairly' important by more than half of the membership but few identified these as the
only ways of being 'truly Scottish'. In short, the table shows that SNP
members acknowledge multiple ways of being Scottish. McCrone has
pointed out: 'The first thing to be said is that in modern Scotland we live
quite happily with multiple meanings of what it means to be a Scot: by
birth, descent and residence' (McCrone, 2001: 156). It appears that this
view is also common amongst SNP members. MacCormick articulated
the relationship between past and present in understanding of the
nation in terms of an 'organic' continuity stemming from 'each generation's own choices' with its crucial and central component being its
name (MacCormick, 1982: 249). In this sense, claiming to be Scots, is
sufficient definition of national identity. Though this articulation is
offered by a leading political philosopher, it encapsulates thinking
within the SNP.

This is clearer when we look at the structure of responses to being 'truly
Scottish'. Table 7.6 reports the proportions of those rating each characteristic in turn as 'very important' (column heading) who also designated
the other characteristics as either 'very' or 'fairly' important (the rows).
These results point to a certain civic–ethnic structure in the data. For
instance, those who described 'to feel Scottish' as 'very important' were
also especially likely to designate 'to respect Scottish political institutions
and laws' as important too. Yet, at the same time, there are numerous
instances in which the distinction is blurred. In particular, these two
civic aspects – respecting Scottish institutions and feeling Scottish – were
also deemed important by those prioritizing the ethnic characteristics.
Equally, while those citing 'being a Christian' as important were disproportionately likely to insist on the ethnic criteria, they were also
concerned by more voluntary aspects such as 'to live in Scotland now'.

Many of the results in Table 7.6 cast doubt on the notion, implicit in
the civic–ethnic dichotomy, that those describing civic characteristics as
important are also inclined to ascribe less importance to ethnic features.
To ascertain whether the characteristics listed are indeed measures of
distinct *dimensions* of national identity, we need to examine the 'internal
structure' of responses to the question, the pattern of covariances
between ratings of the eight characteristics by factor analysis of the
data. There are two broad approaches to factor analysis. One approach
tests whether data conforms to a theoretical prediction about its structure. This tests how closely members' attitudes conform to a civic–ethnic

Table 7.6. Relationships between perceived importance of characteristics for being 'truly Scottish' (%)

	To have Scottish ancestry (22.6%)	To have been born in Scotland (30.8%)	To live in Scotland now (44%)	To have lived in Scotland for most of one's life (26%)	To be a Christian (11.1%)	To respect Scottish political institutions and laws (54.7%)	To feel Scottish (72.1%)	To be able to speak English, Gaelic, or Scots (35.5%)
To have Scottish ancestry	100.0	56.3	32.3	48.2	59.4	27.6	26.3	35.4
To have been born in Scotland	76.7	100.0	43.8	63.5	73.2	36.1	34.5	44.5
To live in Scotland now	62.8	62.5	100.0	80.2	78.0	53.3	50.9	55.5
To have lived in Scotland for most of one's life	55.4	53.6	47.7	100.0	67.3	32.5	31.1	38.5
To be a Christian	29.1	26.4	19.7	28.8	100.0	16.7	13.2	19.1
To respect Scottish political institutions and laws	66.7	64.1	66.2	68.3	82.4	100.0	63.1	71.2
To feel Scottish	83.9	80.7	83.4	86.2	85.8	83.2	100.0	84.4
To be able to speak English, Gaelic, or Scots	55.6	51.3	44.8	52.6	61.1	46.2	41.5	100.0

divide. The second approach is exploratory. A structure that best accounts for the observed covariances is calculated and is then interpreted. Van der Zwet (2010) takes the first approach, testing the SNP membership data against a two-dimensional civic–ethnic measurement model. He concludes that instead of viewing ethnic and civic nationalisms as a dichotomy, the distinction is best understood as two related continuums on which almost all SNP members score high on the civic continuum but a significant number of members also score high on the ethnic continuum, suggesting the two are regarded as non-competitive (van der Zwet, 2010). In the following analysis, we adopt the second approach to factor analysis for two reasons. First, in the absence of precise theoretical expectations about the particular nature and structure of Scottish national identity, we explore patterns rather than test hypotheses. Second, some items are difficult to categorize. Language is a good example. While language can provide a cultural basis for exclusion from a nation, it can also be learned and is therefore less restrictive than criteria such as ancestry and birthplace. This reinforces the importance of context in shaping and limiting the relevance of general theories of national identity.

This analysis involved a principal components analysis (PCA) of responses to the question from Table 7.5. Table 7.7 reports item loadings on the first four factors extracted from the data.[1] Those over 0.4 are highlighted in italic and taken as indicating that the item loads on that factor. The results corroborate van der Zwet's finding (2010) that these

Table 7.7. Factor loadings from PCA of importance ratings of national identity characteristics

How important is ____ to be truly Scottish?	Factor 1	Factor 2	Factor 3	Factor 4
To have Scottish ancestry	*0.912*	−0.029	0.082	0.031
To have been born in Scotland	*0.863*	−0.042	−0.066	0.014
To live in Scotland now	−0.154	0.334	*−0.956*	−0.016
To have lived in Scotland for most of one's life	0.284	0.280	*−0.705*	0.067
To be a Christian	*0.501*	0.229	−0.154	0.002
To respect Scottish political institutions and laws	−0.071	*0.731*	0.027	0.042
To feel Scottish	0.051	*0.701*	−0.039	−0.002
To be able to speak English, Gaelic, or Scots	−0.017	0.341	0.003	*0.969*

[1] In the absence of any reason to suppose the revealed dimensions to be orthogonal, we used Oblimin rotation. Together, the first four factors account for around three-quarters of the variance in the responses. Only the first two meet Kaiser's criterion of an eigenvalue greater than 1.

eight items do not generate a neat two-factor solution. On the one hand, the first two factors might plausibly be described as an ethno-cultural and a civic dimension respectively. Moreover, while 'being a Christian' loads less heavily on the first factor than do the two more 'genealogical' items, it does share considerable variance with them, thus going some way to vindicating the pairing of ethnicity and culture. On the other hand, three of the items do not load at all heavily on either of these factors. The two 'live in Scotland' items (*to live in Scotland now* and *to have lived in Scotland most of one's life*) share very little variance with the other civic characteristics, forming a dimension of their own. In line with earlier arguments, language in this context is a special case and has a factor to itself. Language seems to have virtually nothing to do with ethno-cultural identity but shows some sign of loading on the second factor (perhaps because an unwillingness to learn English is taken as opting out of the civic community in Scotland).

In the light of these results, we proceeded using only the five items that loaded on the first two factors in Table 7.7. They were used to form two summed mini-scales measuring the importance given by respondents to the ethno-cultural and civic dimensions of national identity. The two scales are weakly positively correlated, suggesting that SNP members do not conform to the sharp dichotomy involved in the civic–ethnic distinction. The interrelationship between the two dimensions is clear: most respondents regard the civic characteristics as important; some *also* see ethnic characteristics as important. This suggests that while almost all members see civic characteristics as a necessary condition for being Scottish only some also see those characteristics as a sufficient condition.

These results cast doubt on the value of a sharp distinction between ethnic and civic nationalists. SNP members can indeed be divided into two broad groups. However, while one of these groups has a largely civic conception of Scottishness, the other is civic but also acknowledges an ethnic aspect to this identity. Put another way, SNP members are either 'civic' or 'civic and ethnic' nationalists. There are very few who can be described as ethnic nationalists.

Any dichotomy is an over-simplification and any attempt to divide respondents between the two groups has an arbitrary quality. However, such a division is useful for analysis. Members are categorized as 'civic–ethnic' nationalists if they rated both Scottish ancestry and Scottish birth as 'very' or 'fairly' important. We categorized anyone rating either of these as 'not very' or 'not at all' important as in the 'civic' category. This splits respondents almost fifty–fifty (52 per cent as civic–ethnic, 48 per cent as civic nationalists). What types of people, from what types

Table 7.8. Ethnic–civic conceptions of Scottish identity by socio-demographic variables (%)

	Predominant view of Scottish identity				Predominant view of Scottish identity		
	Civic	Civic–ethnic	N		Civic	Civic–ethnic	N
Age				*Age finished education*			
18–34	62	38	*516*	15 or under	37	63	*1612*
35–44	65	35	*736*	16	45	55	*1131*
45–54	58	42	*1084*	17	51	49	*629*
55–64	55	45	*1641*	18	57	43	*446*
65–74	45	55	*1518*	19 or over	64	36	*2652*
75+	36	64	*925*				
				When joined			
Religion				1930–66	47	53	*741*
None	59	41	*2717*	1967–79	53	47	*1364*
Catholic	58	42	*675*	1980–92	57	43	*1075*
Protestant	42	58	*2625*	1993–2004	53	47	*1511*
Other	60	40	*234*	2005–	50	50	*1567*

of background, adopt a purely civic view of Scottishness? And who maintains that it has an ethnic component? Table 7.8 reports the relationship between these conceptions of national identity and members' socio-demographic characteristics.

Older SNP members were more inclined to perceive an ethnic component to Scottish identity. It is not possible to discern from these data alone whether that is an ageing or a generational effect but the evident non-linearity in the relationship suggests the latter. The period in which a respondent reported first joining the party is more a macro-sociological indicator of the way in which SNP membership may have been driven by different conceptions of Scottish identity over time. It reveals an interesting curvilinear effect. The tendency for earlier joiners to see an ethnic component to national identity is in line with the age differences discussed above, but the more recent upturn to almost the same level in the ethnic conception is less easily explained. As the relative youth of new members is dampening that effect, the upturn would seem even more striking when we control for age. Although 'to be a Christian' was excluded from the categorization of ethnic and civic nationalists, there are some quite pronounced differences by religious affiliation, with an ethnic conception of identity weakest among those disclaiming any religious affiliation and among non-Christian SNP members and strongest among those identifying with the Church of Scotland.

Conclusion

The empirical evidence presented in this chapter has implications for much of the theoretical writings on civic and ethnic nationalism. The origins of the distinction lie in normative efforts to distinguish between 'good' and 'bad' nationalisms. Application of these terms in debates pursues a similar purpose, whether it is the SNP's efforts to present itself as a liberal nationalist party or some of its opponents' efforts to suggest illiberal tendencies. In reality, the SNP is civic in the sense that its policies are amongst the most liberal of any mainstream party in the United Kingdom on citizenship, emigration, and multiculturalism. Additionally, very few of its members would define Scottishness in exclusive ethnic terms. The SNP members accept a plurality of ways of defining belonging to the Scottish nation. Moreover, one-fifth of the party members acknowledge some element of a British identity. The membership as a whole is therefore more pluralist than the leadership in this respect in acknowledging a British identity, echoing a point made in the previous chapter about the strength of Scottish identity – like the commitment to independence – being strongest amongst those more active in the party.

On the whole, however, this plurality conforms with the party's formal position. Activists reflect the leadership's line in rejecting an exclusively ethnic definition of nationality and are willing to acknowledge many ways of defining who belongs to the Scottish nation, including an ethnic definition of belonging. This has allowed the SNP leadership to follow a liberal policy on citizenship and advocate increasing immigration into Scotland without fear of a backlash from its members.

8

Independence, Policies, and Strategies

Introduction

In this chapter, we explore members' opinions of the SNP's (Scottish National Party) policies, in particular views on Scotland's constitutional status, and attitudes on how the SNP should pursue its goals. Nationalism is not only one of social science's 'contested concepts' (Gallie, 1956) but 'politics is deeply implicated in issues of [its] definition' (Özkirimli, 2005: 15). Gellner's notion that nationalism is a political principle, which holds that the 'political and national units should be congruent' (Gellner, 1983: 1) is, at best, a starting point. It raises questions as to how SNP members conceive of statehood. What does independence mean today? Under Gellner's definition, Scottish nationalists might support a Scottish Parliament within the United Kingdom or support independence outside or within the European Union (EU). Since the party's foundation, there has been a tension between those supporting different versions of independence. In large measure, this comes down to the external support system in which an independent Scotland should operate: its relations with the rest of the United Kingdom, especially England; its relations with wider international bodies, including the British Empire in the early part of the SNP's history and the EU today; and its relation with the defence community, if any, most notably deciding whether to support membership of the North Atlantic Treaty Organization (NATO). In addition, as we saw in Chapter 2, there has also been an enduring debate on whether, and if so where, the SNP places itself on the left–right and liberal–authoritarian spectrums. Having members elected to public office, whether as local councillors, Members of Parliament (MPs), Members of the European Parliament (MEPs), or Members of the Scottish Parliament (MSPs) has required the SNP to develop positions on contemporary public policy concerns. This chapter considers the party's views on the kinds of issues that are debated and decided in these representative institutions.

Scotand's constitutional status

The overwhelming majority of SNP members opt for independence as their first constitutional preference (Table 8.1). However, independence is not the first choice of around one in eight SNP members. Most of this minority would prefer that the Scottish Parliament had 'more powers', although over three-quarters of these members opt for independence as their second preference. Additionally, roughly a quarter of those who support independence would prefer to see Scotland outside the EU. This might seem strange given that 'independence in Europe' has been the central objective of the SNP for more than twenty years. However, there has long been an anti-European integration element within the party and at times in its past the party was officially hostile to membership of the European Communities (Lynch, 1996; Mitchell, 1998). The second choices of those who opt for independence in Europe are split evenly between independence outside Europe and more powers for the Scottish Parliament. It has been commonly assumed that attitudes on Scotland's constitutional status operate along a continuum from independence outside the EU, through independence in Europe, more powers, the status quo to the status quo ante. This appears to be an oversimplification with the European dimension operating as a separate, if related, attitudinal spectrum. Many supporters of further devolution might be expected, in a simple continuous spectrum, to be more likely to give independence in the EU as second preference rather than independence

Table 8.1. First and second preferences on the constitutional issue (%)

	First preference	Second preference			
		Independent within EU	Independent outside EU	Further devolution	N
Independent within EU	65	–	46	54	3941
Independent outside EU	22	77	–	23	1313
Further devolution	12	76	24	–	707
Status quo	1				
Status quo ante	0				
N	6121				

outside the EU. However, a quarter of those who gave more powers as their first preference gave independence outside Europe as second preference.

In exploring the sources of these differences, we have identified which groups of members are most/least likely to support the party's flagship policy of independence in Europe. A striking finding is that women are more likely than men to report 'more powers' as first preference, though this is still very much a minority view amongst women (Table 8.2). As this difference is also evident in the electorate as a whole and in voting behaviour, with women less likely to vote SNP than men, the party's flagship policy may be part of the problem (Johns et al., 2010). The age differences in constitutional preferences are wider, and are consistent with the traditional characterization of support for independence as youthful radicalism. Over 90 per cent of members under 35 ranked one of the independence options as their top preference. Once more, these differences broadly reflect the pattern in the Scottish population as a whole.

The 'radical youth' hypothesis may provide a life-cycle explanation for the age differences in Table 8.2. However, elsewhere in this book we

Table 8.2. Constitutional preferences by sex, age, and time of joining party (%)

	First preference			N (min.)
	Independent inside EU	Independent outside EU	More powers	
Sex				
Male	69	22	9	*4058*
Female	60	23	17	*1933*
Age (year)				
18–34	74	19	6	*479*
35–44	74	19	7	*687*
45–54	71	18	11	*978*
55–64	66	23	11	*1510*
65–74	63	23	15	*1386*
75+	55	28	18	*840*
When joined				
1930–66	62	30	9	*662*
1967–79	67	22	11	*1233*
1980–92	69	22	9	*983*
1993–2004	68	20	13	*1403*
2005–	65	21	14	*1448*
National identity				
Scottish only	68	23	9	*4569*
Some British	60	18	23	*1126*

have stressed generational explanations – that is, when respondents joined the party rather than how old they are now – for differences in values and attitudes within the SNP membership. Apart from the tendency for members who joined the party before the United Kingdom's accession to the European Communities to be less committed to EU membership, the cohort differences in first preferences are small. The most radical cohort – defined as those least willing to compromise on independence – is of those joining in the 1980s and the most willing to compromise are the newest recruits though the difference is not great. Younger party members are most in line with official SNP policy of supporting Independence in the EU. However, there is less difference between members on constitutional preference according to when someone joined the SNP though some evidence of increased support for more powers amongst those who joined in the lead up to and since devolution. This last finding is interesting as the SNP has placed greater emphasis on making devolution work and, at least implicitly, on 'furthering Scottish interests' as distinct from its constitutional policy, but this has hardly been reflected in the party membership's constitutional preference. Independence remains the prime motivation in joining, being active, and remaining a member of the party. Those disclaiming any British identification are more likely to favour independence, either in or out of the EU. Among the much smaller group describing themselves as at least partly British, support for independence was less strong than amongst those who disclaimed any British identity.

The meaning of independence

The survey results tell us the proportion of members supporting options frequently used in research on public attitudes. However, behind these headline constitutional options lie a variety of detailed positions. The meaning of Scottish independence and the manner in which it is brought about have been the subject of serious academic and journalistic analysis (Murkens et al., 2002; Keating, 2009) yet little of this has been incorporated into analysis of public opinion. A number of senior members of the SNP have engaged with these questions. Neil MacCormick, former SNP Member of the European Parliament and Vice President of the party, wrote on the subject at length especially in discussing Scottish membership of the EU (MacCormick, 1999, 2000). Shortly before the 2007 elections, two senior party members, later Cabinet Ministers in the SNP Government, wrote books that addressed the meaning and means towards its achievement (MacAskill, 2004; MacLeod and

Russell, 2006). Amongst the issues raised by Kenny MacAskill was whether an independent Scotland would share services and institutions with its neighbours:

> Is there a need for a separate DVLA or even Ordnance Survey?...Does a bureaucracy need to be created in Saltcoats as well as in Swansea? Can we not simply pay our share as well as our respects? Do we need to reinvent the Civil Aviation Authority or other such Institutions as opposed to exercising control from north of the border even if the Institution remains located in the south of it...There are numerous other organisations and Departments where separation is not necessary but the right to direct and instruct is. (MacAskill, 2004: 29–30)

Mike Russell and his co-author, in their book, argued for a 'new union' as a first step towards independence. This was unusual language given that the term 'new union' had been used in the past by a variety of opponents of the SNP and implied a revived union rather than a step towards independence. Russell and MacAskill were each articulating a nuanced understanding of independence beyond the headline notions.

We explored attitudes towards independence in our interviews. The key aspects of this were Scotland's relations with the rest of the United Kingdom and with other states and polities but there was also some discussion of whether independence had non-constitutional meanings. Specifying how relations with the rest of the United Kingdom would or would not be affected by independence was a major theme for many senior members. The SNP has long argued that it supports a 'social union' meaning the family, personal, and professional links within the United Kingdom that would remain unaffected by constitutional independence. Freedom of movement of people, in effect, would be unaffected by independence. The term 'social union' has since been used more narrowly by the Calman Commission, established by the SNP's opponents following the 2007 elections, in referring to 'some common expectations about social welfare' (Calman, 2009: 6). Calman maintained that, 'We think that there are certain social rights which should also be substantially the same, even when it is best that they are separately run in Scotland. The most important of these are that access to health care and education should be, as now, essentially free and provided at the point of need' (Ibid.). This is a very different, and much more restrictive, understanding of 'social union' from that which has been used previously. Senior SNP members agreed that these common social rights might exist well beyond the United Kingdom and stressed the differences, including different expectations of social welfare that fed into demands for devolution. In defining how Scotland diverged from the rest of Britain, they looked back to the period when the Conservatives were last in power and ahead to the prospect of the Conservatives returning to power as creating the conditions under which divergence was most obvious. Indeed, the experience of 'Thatcherism' was important for many of those interviewed either in bringing them into the party, forging their political outlook, or encouraging political activity.

The 'DVLA Question', in reference to MacAskill's question whether there was a need for a seperate Driver and Vehicle Licensing Agency, was put to all senior members, that is, whether they accepted that there should be shared public services and institutions and, if so, what these might include. Only a very small number took the view that sharing public services and institutions was unacceptable and almost all of these accepted that transitional arrangements involving shared services and institutions might be necessary. However, most senior members were pragmatic, including some who had in the recent past been seen as hardliners. A commonly used analogy was with practice in business and local government when contracts for providing services were drawn up or when joint action and shared services were possible. Examples given ranged from cooperation in dealing with swine flu and foot-and-mouth disease through to defence procurement. The only hesitation came from some members who were concerned that paying for a service provided elsewhere would result in job losses in Scotland.

Economic, monetary, and fiscal independence was understood in equally pragmatic terms. There was no support for a separate Scottish currency. A number of senior members dismissed concerns that the lack of a Scottish currency would mean Scotland was not really independent. One MSP asked rhetorically whether Ireland was not independent for the fifty years it shared a currency with Britain. The issue on the currency was between whether Scotland should stay with the pound sterling or join the Euro zone and, if the latter, when this should happen. Once more, views on joining the Euro were pragmatic. Predictably perhaps, there was less emotional attachment to sterling than is evident in other parties in the United Kingdom. It was acknowledged that the absence of a Scottish currency might limit Scotland's economic independence but the response was almost invariably that Scotland was part of a 'globalized' or 'interdependent' world. Indeed, a few senior members ventured to suggest that there was 'no such thing as independence' but were quick to insert a caveat along the lines of 'as sometimes/usually understood'. As we saw in Chapter 2, the SNP had openly debated membership of the EU in the past. By the time of this study, it appeared that there were few, if any, remnants amongst the party's elites of the old position associated with former deputy leader, Jim Fairlie, who saw EU membership as undermining meaningful independence. While there was criticism of individual EU policies, there was overwhelming support for Scottish membership of the EU. One MSP, previously associated with a fundamentalist position maintained that 'Independence could not be a Year Zero' and that the SNP 'couldn't start afresh but had to work within existing obligations'. What emerged was an idea of independence that was little different from confederation, in how these members saw Scotland's relations with both the rest of the United Kingdom and the EU developing.

What has also emerged amongst the elites is a view that independence needs to be defined in non-constitutional terms and that the party's socio-economic ideology needs to be related to its constitutional aims. Related to this, and conforming with the findings discussed in Chapter 7, were frequent references relating independence to self-confidence by senior members. Building the self-confidence of individuals and local communities as well as in Scotland as a whole was a theme of many interviews.

Left or right?

The SNP has characterized itself as a 'moderate left of centre' party since the early 1980s (Mitchell, 1996: 232). During the years of Margaret Thatcher's premiership, the party edged further leftwards. The party's view of itself as left of centre became further ingrained as Labour moved rightwards. Left and right are relative terms and descriptions of the SNP as left-wing commonly attempts to place it relative to the Labour Party. Therefore, questions on where SNP members positioned themselves and the party are most meaningful when compared with how they see other parties, especially the Labour Party. Respondents were asked to place themselves and the major British parties, including the SNP, on a scale from 0 (left) to 10 (right). Figure 8.1 shows where members placed themselves and the party on the spectrum. Both sets of placements are slightly skewed to the left but both peak at the midpoint of the scale. While some members hold a rather more extreme position than they attribute to the SNP, the ideological centres of gravity of the party and its membership appear very close together, just to the left of centre.

One reason for such apparent proximity is that scale placements such as these are highly susceptible to *assimilation* bias (Markus and Converse, 1979; Merrill et al., 2001). Rather than locating themselves and their preferred party independently, people tend to project their own

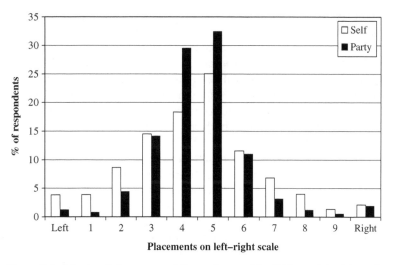

Figure 8.1. Members' placements of themselves and the SNP on a left–right scale

position onto their party or to infer their own position from the party. The results in the left-hand panel of Table 8.3 suggest considerable bias along those lines. The SNP was placed on the left (i.e. anywhere left of the midpoint on the scale) by almost four-fifths of those who placed themselves on the left but by only one-fifth of those placing themselves on the right. Assimilation's obverse is *contrast*, whereby respondents exaggerate the distance between themselves and a competitor party. The results for Labour placements also indicate the effects of that bias. Labour was placed on the right by three-quarters of those placing themselves on the left but by less than half of those who placed themselves on the right.

The patterns in Table 8.4 reflect the link between Scottish and left-wing identities that were forged strongly during the Thatcher years. These results illustrate how placements of self, the SNP, and Labour vary with the period when respondents joined the SNP. Each set of

Table 8.3. Summary of left–right placements of SNP and Labour by self-placement (%)

Self-placements	SNP placements			Labour placements			N (min.)
	Left	Centre	Right	Left	Centre	Right	
Left	78	17	5	15	12	73	2952
Centre	25	65	10	30	9	61	1455
Right	21	31	48	37	16	48	1497

Table 8.4. Summary of left–right placements of selves, the SNP, and Labour by time of joining party (%)

When joined	Self-placements			SNP placements			Labour placements			N (min.)
	Left	Centre	Right	Left	Centre	Right	Left	Centre	Right	
1930–66	47	28	25	50	34	16	29	11	61	690
1967–79	50	26	24	53	32	15	23	11	67	1265
1980–92	56	23	22	57	29	14	17	12	71	1008
1993–2004	51	24	25	49	33	18	23	12	65	1385
2005–	43	26	31	44	33	23	28	15	57	1372

data shows the same curve. Members who joined the SNP during the 1980s are most likely to see themselves and their party as left-wing and most likely to see Labour as right-wing. Those who joined more recently are more similar to those who joined more than four decades ago, before the party's rise to political relevance, and are subjectively the most right-wing cohort of all.

These scale placements give insights into how members think about themselves, their party and its rivals. However, they have limitations as measures of ideology. Not only are there problems of bias, as described above, but they also tell us little about respondents' opinions on particular issues and policies. As ideology is a basic structure for individual beliefs, it is common to measure it by asking a series of specific policy questions. Evans et al. (1996) have developed batteries of agree–disagree statements to measure left–right and libertarian–authoritarian values, arguing that these are the main dimensions structuring political attitudes in the British public. These batteries, alongside a wide range of other opinion questions, were included in the SNP membership survey. Table 8.5 reports members' responses to the items intended to measure (economic) left–right attitudes. Broadly speaking, these corroborate the story of a centre-left party told by the self-placements. Comfortable majorities of the members are in favour of redistribution of wealth, oppose cutting public spending in order to cut tax, and are doubtful that the less well off get a fair deal. However, there are clear limits to these left-wing inclinations, with half of the members agreeing that it is not government's responsibility to provide jobs for all and only one-third disagreeing that private enterprise is the best solution to economic problems.

The questions developed by Evans et al. (1996) have been widely used in surveys of social attitudes and the three items asterisked in Table 8.5 were included in the Scottish Social Attitudes survey of 2007. By forming these three items into a short index of left–right attitudes for that

Table 8.5. Agree–disagree responses on left–right attitude items (%)

	Strongly agree	Agree	Neither	Disagree	Strongly disagree	N
Working people get their fair share of the nation's wealth	11	17	18	40	16	*6754*
*There is one law for the rich and one law for the poor	25	41	19	12	3	*6728*
Private enterprise is the best way to solve Britain's economic problems	7	22	38	26	8	*6681*
*Government should redistribute income from the better off to the less well off	20	44	22	12	2	*6705*
It is not government's responsibility to provide a job for everyone who wants one	8	39	19	29	6	*6658*
*Management will always try to get the better of employees if it gets the chance	14	40	23	20	4	*6711*
The government should reduce spending on public services in order to cut taxes	3	10	16	52	19	*6702*

survey and our own, and then dividing that scale at equal intervals so as to divide respondents into five groups, we can compare SNP members with the party's voters and the electorate as a whole. The picture that emerges is shown in Figure 8.2. Each of the three groups leans to the left rather than to the right. However, SNP members are slightly more left-wing than SNP voters and appreciably more so than the Scottish electorate.

Libertarian or authoritarian?

Another battery of questions attempts to measure libertarian–authoritarian values. Table 8.6 reports the results. As the average age of SNP members is high and as authoritarian attitudes are substantially more common among older people, especially from the pre-1960s generations, we might expect a fairly authoritarian membership independent of the party's stance on these issues (Tilley, 2005). The large proportion agreeing that young people have insufficient respect for traditional values and one in five members condemning all homosexual relations may say as much about the age of the party's members as about their politics. However, the key finding is the mixed picture that emerges. Members are in favour of tougher prison sentences but more than half

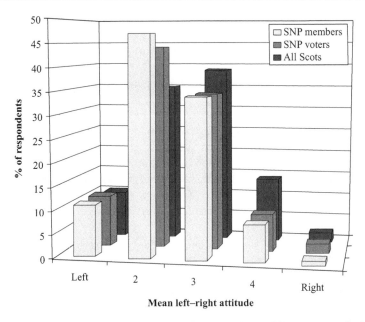

Figure 8.2. Left–right attitude scores: SNP members; SNP voters; and the electorate

Table 8.6. Agree–disagree responses on libertarian–authoritarian attitude items (%)

	Strongly agree	Agree	Neither	Disagree	Strongly disagree	N
*People who break the law should be given stiffer sentences	33	30	27	9	1	6768
*Young people today don't have enough respect for traditional values	26	37	22	13	2	6789
The death penalty is never justified, even for very serious crimes	28	23	11	24	14	6792
Homosexual relations are always wrong	10	11	27	25	27	6706
Censorship of films and magazines have no place in a free society	14	25	16	38	8	6712
In principle, identity cards are a good idea	8	26	11	21	34	6657
*The law should always be obeyed, even if a particular law is wrong	7	29	21	36	7	6694

oppose the death penalty. They are split on censorship and whether to obey a 'bad' law. Identity cards, despite a close association with the last UK Labour Government, receive some support as well as some stiff opposition.

A clearer picture may emerge from comparisons with SNP voters and the Scottish electorate as a whole. The three asterisked items in Table 8.6 were included in election surveys in 2007. The results are shown in Figure 8.3. SNP members are more libertarian than both SNP voters and the wider electorate. This may seem surprising given their average age; on the other hand, the membership is also disproportionately educated and education, especially at university level, tends to foster a more libertarian outlook (Schuman et al., 1992). So, if age and education cancel one another out, the SNP's membership appears to have a fairly moderate opinion profile on these issues.

The analysis so far suggests that members' ideological identities vary, and not in a simple linear manner, depending on their 'cohort', that is, the period in which they joined the party. The left–right and libertarian–authoritarian scales offer an economical means of testing whether the same is true of attitudes on policy. The left-hand panel of Table 8.7 gives

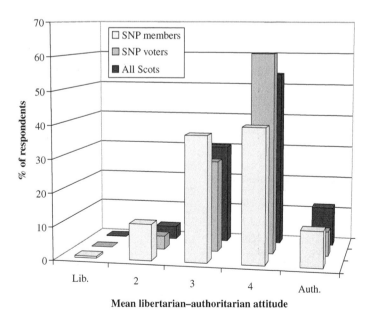

Figure 8.3. Libertarian–authoritarian attitude scores: SNP members; SNP voters; and the electorate

Table 8.7. Mean left–right and libertarian–authoritarian scale scores by time of joining party

When joined	Raw means		Means controlling for age		N (min.)
	Left–right	Libertarian–authoritarian	Left–right	Libertarian–authoritarian	
1930–66	2.38	3.53	2.42	3.43	789
1967–79	2.41	3.42	2.43	3.37	1420
1980–92	2.39	3.40	2.38	3.41	1122
1993–2004	2.45	3.50	2.44	3.52	1580
2005–	2.41	3.57	2.40	3.63	1633
F (sig.)	1.54 (n.s.)	9.67 (<0.01)	1.16 (n.s.)	19.45 (<0.01)	

the mean scores on the two scales by cohort. We also report F-ratios, which test for significant differences between the means (i.e. whether variations within each column are likely to be genuine cohort differences in attitudes rather than just random fluctuations). The left–right scores in the first column barely vary, and this is confirmed by the non-significant F-ratio. In short, while these groups may think of themselves differently when it comes to the abstract left–right scale, their views on economic left–right issues are broadly the same. The libertarian–authoritarian mean scores vary a little more. Those who joined most recently are slightly more authoritarian than those who joined before 1967 despite, for the most part, being much younger. This point highlights the need to take age into account. The right-hand panel of the table shows the mean attitude scores statistically controlling for members' age.[1] There remains no significant difference in left–right scores, but the pattern of less libertarian attitudes, especially in that latest cohort, becomes clearer. As little in the party's recent discourse can explain this trend, it may simply reflect changes in Scottish society in general.

In the 1980s, support for a Scottish Parliament grew with the perception that the Conservatives, with little and declining support in Scotland, were anti-Scottish. This encouraged an equation of Scottish interests with left-wing politics. Constitutional preferences, national identity, and party choice were linked in many voters' minds (Mitchell and Bennie, 1996). This background may contribute to explaining the views of SNP members. Those who placed themselves on the left were more likely to favour independence (Table 8.8). However, this occurs only so far as left–right self-placements are concerned. There is less evidence of left-wing opinion

---

[1] These statistics are the result of an analysis of variance with cohort as a fixed factor and age as a covariate.

generating support for independence when scores on policy positions are considered. Research suggests that political identity is more important than policy preferences in determining voting behaviour (Sears et al., 1980; Curtice, 2006) and it appears that this is also true for constitutional preferences amongst SNP members. There is, however, evidence that policy attitudes on the libertarian–authoritarian spectrum relate strongly to constitutional preferences. The pattern mirrors that shown by the left–right self-placements, with authoritarian respondents disproportionately likely to oppose independence but also, if they do support independence, to prefer that option outside the EU. This suggests a link between exclusively Scottish identity, left-wing self-perception and libertarian attitudes with this cluster of SNP members most likely to support independence in the EU. These findings from the membership data are also evident in the elite interviews where senior members conformed broadly with the same constellation of attitudes.

Other policy views

Many of the issues on which parties, especially governing parties, are required to make decisions do not fall along either of the two dimensions that we have looked at so far. Responses on miscellaneous policy questions are summarized in Table 8.9. The first three questions focus on environmental policy. In common with the wider public, SNP members are more likely to acknowledge environmental concerns, with only one in four agreeing that 'we worry too much about the environment', than willing to endorse specific policies to address these concerns, for example, there is limited appetite for higher taxes on car owners. Most members share the party's long-standing opposition to nuclear energy though more recent recruits to the party are less opposed to nuclear power but still more than half of those who joined after 2005 oppose it.

Another controversial issue and the source of some friction within the party has been NATO membership. Although party policy supports withdrawal, more than half of the members regard membership as in Scotland's interests. However, while members broadly support NATO membership, few feel strongly about it. At first glance, the members' willingness to criticize the EU also seems at variance with the party's strongly pro-European stance. However, neither point should be overstated. The party elites have been highly critical of aspects of EU policy, especially in fisheries policy. In sum, the party's elite and mass membership may have slightly different perspectives on international affairs but there is no evidence of a major clash of views.

Table 8.8. Constitutional preferences by national identity and left–right/libertarian–authoritarian attitudes (%)

	First preference			First/second preferences		N (min.)
	Independent inside EU	Independent outside EU	More powers	Independent either way	Other	
Left–right self-placement						
Left	74	19	7	58	42	2657
Centre	65	21	14	50	50	1367
Right	58	26	16	50	50	1386
Left–right attitudes						
Left	66	23	12	53	47	3424
Centre	67	21	12	51	49	2075
Right	64	21	14	50	50	508
Libertarian–authoritarian attitudes						
Libertarian	79	16	5	58	42	692
Centre	74	18	8	58	42	2265
Authoritarian	57	26	16	46	54	3047

Table 8.9. Agree–disagree responses on miscellaneous policy issues (%)

	Strongly agree	Agree	Neither	Disagree	Strongly disagree	N
We worry too much about the environment and not enough about prices and jobs	6	20	26	36	12	6706
For the sake of the environment, car users should pay higher taxes	7	24	22	33	13	6763
Nuclear energy is essential for future prosperity	6	14	17	31	33	6721
Membership of NATO is in Scotland's strategic interest	14	39	24	15	8	6750
The European Union has become too centralized	24	36	24	14	2	6724
Separate Catholic schools should be phased out	36	29	18	11	7	6809
The monarchy has no place in a modern democracy	35	22	23	14	6	6800

One issue on which there is a significant difference between the leadership and members is faith schools. Almost two-thirds of members would like to see separate Catholic schools phased out and a similar proportion favours an end to state subsidy for private education. Moreover, many members feel strongly on these matters, especially the Catholic schools issue. Yet the party shows no interest in changing the status of private schools and its commitment to denominational education remains strong. This reflects the situation in Scotland as a whole where the political elites, across all parties, have long accepted separate Catholic schools while the public has supported an integrated educational system. There was almost no support for the integration of the educational system in elite interviews though the reasoning differed amongst the elite. For the most part, Catholic schools were accepted pragmatically but there was a significant body of opinion, especially amongst the party's most senior members, that Catholic schools should be supported in principle in recognition of Scottish society's religious pluralism.

Another issue on which the leadership and official policy is at variance with the membership is the monarchy, as indicated in Table 8.9. Almost 60 per cent of members believe that there is no place in a modern democracy for the monarchy while only one in five disagrees with this view. Again, there was more support for the monarch in the elite interviews though there was little evidence of principled support. In 1977, the Queen had commented in her Silver Jubilee Address that, 'I cannot forget that I was crowned Queen of the United Kingdom of Great Britain and Northern Ireland.' This was taken at the time to be an attack on the SNP, then riding high in the opinion polls. Gordon Wilson, SNP MP at the time, described the Address as the Queen 'intervening in domestic politics on behalf of the unionist cause' (Wilson, 2009: 133). The party's response at the time had been defensive, insisting that it wanted to end the Union of Parliaments, not the Union of Crowns. As discussed in Chapter 2, after the SNP lost nine of its eleven seats two years later, the '79 Group' was set up within the party with three aims: independence; socialism; and republicanism. This was in part a response to the monarch's intervention. However, the party rejected moves to adopt republicanism at annual conferences. There was evidence from elite interviews that there is some sympathy for republicanism amongst senior members but few see it as a priority. One MSP summed up the views of many colleagues when he described his republicanism: 'I accept it is not up top on my list of priorities. It's number a zillion – there are far more important things that need to be sorted. That doesn't mean I am a monarchist – just a realist.'

Differences such as those on faith schools and the monarchy are the exception rather than the rule, however. There is little evidence that the leadership has much to cause it alarm from party members. The membership is, as the party has long styled itself, moderate left of centre on economic issues. In any case, on both left–right and libertarian–authoritarian issues, the median SNP member is not far from the median voter, such that the party leadership already has an electoral incentive to give members what they want. Considering that members are by definition disproportionately engaged politically, the widespread avoidance of the 'strongly' positioned categories on some of the more controversial questions is noteworthy. The bulk of the membership seems neither very radical on, nor much roused by, many of the issues considered here. Of course, this might all be expected given that, as we saw in Chapter 5, a different set of concerns and passions brought members into the party.

Party strategy

As discussed in Chapter 2, the key tension within the SNP over the years leading to devolution was that between its pragmatic and fundamentalist wings. In the concluding section of this chapter, we assess party members' attitudes on strategy. Our starting point is a list of agree–disagree items on party strategy (Table 8.10). Responses to the first statement show that SNP members remain committed to independence but other results point to widespread acceptance of pragmatic means of achieving this goal. There is a general willingness to cooperate, compromise and accept devolution. Only one in five members rejected the proposition that independence should sometimes need to take second place. These responses constitute clear endorsement of the leadership's strategy of working within the current arrangements. More formal pacts with other parties were slightly less popular but were favoured on balance. The lukewarm support for coalitions may have been because the SNP had formed a minority government at the time of the survey and was riding high in the opinion polls. There is little evidence of a potential for a fundamentalist backlash against devolution. More broadly, these findings are in line with the profile of the membership built up so far in this book pointing to a pragmatic set of attitudes that extends to willingness to cooperate with the other major parties.

Amid this consensus, it is worth looking at the factors driving any disagreement that exists. As with left–right and libertarian–authoritarian attitudes, we simplify the analysis by forming a short scale based on

Table 8.10. Agree–disagree responses on party strategy (%)

	Strongly agree	Agree	Neither	Disagree	Strongly disagree	N
*The SNP's primary goal is independence and all else should be secondary	38	33	11	16	2	6707
To achieve the ultimate goal of independence, the SNP should concentrate on making devolution work	36	50	9	4	1	6712
To achieve independence the SNP must be prepared to work with other parties and organizations	30	60	8	2	0	6748
*The SNP's primary goal is independence but this may need to take second place when other matters arise affecting Scotland	14	51	15	16	4	6690
The creation of a Scottish Parliament with devolved powers makes independence more difficult to achieve for the SNP	4	12	16	50	18	6707
Participating in a governing coalition in the Scottish Parliament would involve the SNP compromising on its goal of independence	7	26	23	36	8	6672
The SNP should always stand by its principles even if this loses votes	30	51	12	7	1	6743
*The SNP should put effort into exploring pacts with other parties, even if this involves policy compromises	4	43	26	23	3	6696
The SNP should spend less time creating a professional media image, and put more effort into promoting its programme and policies	11	30	35	22	3	6696

three items – those asterisked in Table 8.10 – which are the core of debates on strategy.[2] The latter two statements are reverse-scored such that the scale runs from 1 to 5. However, so few respondents fell into either of the outside categories that we collapsed either side of the middle category to form a three-category scale: pragmatic; uncertain; and fundamentalist. Table 8.11 shows how the distribution of members among these categories depends on a range of likely influences.

Beginning in the right-hand part of the table, we can see that the more 'fundamentalist' national identity – 'Scottish not British' – is associated with more uncompromising views on party strategy. There are only limited differences by left–right self-placement. Those whose first preference is for further devolution are more likely to support a pragmatic approach. Independence outside the EU looks the most fundamentalist position. However, the most striking feature of the constitutional preference analysis is how small the differences are. Even though two of the three questions making up the pragmatist–fundamentalist index were about independence, the correlation between constitutional preference and that index is not especially strong.

There is further encouraging news for the party leadership in the left-hand panel of the table. The SNP's youngest members and newest recruits are noticeably the most pragmatic. While socialization may take these newer members in another direction, on the whole these results point to a membership likely to become increasingly pragmatic. They also suggest that the party's approach to independence has not only been accepted by existing members but also attracted new ones. The scale of the cohort differences is significant and is greater than the corresponding differences on constitutional preferences (see Table 8.11). In other words, the pragmatist orientation of new members cannot simply be accounted for by their being less likely to support independence. Even those new members who remain committed to independence are distinctive in their willingness to endorse a pragmatic approach. Of course, it is not unusual for a party's membership to be satisfied with a successful leadership's strategy. Disquiet and defiance – in this case concerning a perceived dilution of the commitment to independence – are more likely among what might be a relatively small stratum of activists and likely to grow after an electoral defeat or setback.

[2] This scale shows adequate internal consistency (Cronbach's alpha = 0.43, respectable for a three-item index).

Table 8.11. Fundamentalist–pragmatist stance by age, cohort, identities, and attitudes (%)

	Pragmatist	Uncertain	Fundamentalist	N		Pragmatist	Uncertain	Fundamentalist	N
Age (year)									
18–34	55	15	30	522					
35–44	47	17	36	747					
45–54	47	16	37	1104					
55–64	45	17	38	1690					
					National identity				
					Scottish only	43	18	40	5159
					Some British	58	17	24	1262
65–74	47	18	35	1571					
75+	40	20	40	987					
					Left–right self-placement				
					Left	42	17	41	2981
					Centre	50	17	33	1528
					Right	48	18	34	1568
When joined									
1930–66	34	16	50	780	*Constitutional preference*				
1967–79	41	19	40	1400	Independent inside EU	46	18	37	3945
1980–92	43	18	39	1104	Independent outside EU	41	16	43	1311
1993–2004	50	16	34	1556	More powers	58	19	24	707
2005–	55	17	28	1616					

Conclusion

As Derek Urwin noted, there is always a tension between those willing to 'settle in the medium term for something less – for example, some form of limited autonomy or devolution, something that might strike a chord with more voters – and a more rigid nationalism of anything short of full independence'. However, he noted that involvement in the political system makes members 'more moderate, more willing perhaps to accept political compromise' (Urwin, 1994: 11). This tension exists in many parties seeking radical change, whether constitutional or economic and social in nature. The SNP suggests that the tension can be exaggerated or, at least, is contextually dependent. As we saw in Chapter 2, deep divisions were manifest at SNP conferences in the period after heavy defeats in 1979. The survey on which this study is based was conducted in a very different context, shortly after the SNP became Scotland's largest party and formed a government for the first time in its history. There is evidence of differences within the party but a clear consensus around support for independence in Europe and support for a pragmatic approach to achieving this goal.

There also appears to be evidence of consensus around a moderate left of centre policy agenda. The SNP appears to be a fairly conventional political party which has developed a reasonably clear ideological position on issues associated with the left–right spectrum of politics though appears less coherent on the libertarian–authoritarian spectrum. The survey only offers a snapshot of opinion at a given period in time but there is evidence that its most recent recruits are more pragmatic, less left-wing, and less libertarian than earlier cohorts. As these are also characteristics of the electorate as a whole – and especially SNP voters – this could simply be the consequence of the party expanding its membership beyond the traditional base. Whether this has implications for the party's future policy direction is unclear. For one thing, it depends on the extent to which socialization within the party brings these newer members closer into line with the party's traditional thinking and policies. In any case, the extent to which this new generation differs from those who joined in the past should not be exaggerated.

9

Conclusion

This book is a contribution to our understanding of the Scottish National Party (SNP). We have examined its membership, structure, ideology, and beliefs and set these into the wider context of debates on political participation and political parties. The book challenges a number of well-established myths about the party. These myths were inferred from its electoral support and based on the public image of the party projected at conferences, at election times, and by its leaders. This fragmentary evidence was combined with existing knowledge of other political parties, especially those operating in the same electoral arenas as the SNP, to offer a picture of the party. The two most striking differences between the evidence accumulated here and the myths of the SNP are its gender and age compositions.

The SNP has long been a party in which women have held prominent positions. Winnie Ewing's election in 1967 as an SNP MP marked the beginning of the modern phase of Scottish nationalism. She entered the very male world of Scottish politics. The party has boasted a number of high-profile senior women over subsequent years: Margo MacDonald; Isobel Lindsay; Jeannette Jones; Margaret Ewing; Roseanna Cunningham; and Nicola Sturgeon. Indeed, in the 1970s, it was not unknown for opponents to attack the SNP as the 'women's party'. Tam Dalyell, Labour MP and leading opponent of the SNP and devolution, argued that women, who 'tend to be more emotional about their politics than men', were the main supporters of a Scottish Parliament (Dalyell, 1977: 224).

There were only forty-one women MPs returned from Scottish constituencies between 1923 and 2010 (Kenny and Mackay 2010), of whom six (14.6 per cent) have been SNP Members, a far higher proportion than the SNP's contingent of MPs would have suggested. If any party might have been expected to have provided a role model for women's advancement, then it was the SNP. Yet, the membership of the SNP is overwhelmingly male. Indeed, the proportion of women members who have joined most recently has fallen back to levels recorded before the SNP had its breakthrough with Winnie Ewing's election in 1967, at least as evidenced by the proportion of members who remain in the party from that period. The party not only attracts fewer women than men to its membership but also attracts a higher proportion of male than female voters. Only twelve of the SNP's forty-seven MSPs elected in 2007 were women. The SNP's women have distinct views. They tend to be less radical in their politics than men, less willing to support independence, less willing to put themselves forward for party office and they tend to be more focused on local level activities, party functions, and fundraising rather than formal decision-making positions.

The idea of the SNP as a young person's party had been evident in election surveys, at least until recently, and the party's image as an energetic youthful party was well established in its campaigns in the 1960s and 1970s. However, the membership survey shows the SNP to be an ageing party. The youthful generation that joined in the 1970s, some of whom drifted away and have recently rejoined the party, remain the party's bedrock today. Fewer than 8 per cent of members are below 35 and are considerably outnumbered by those over 75. The SNP may recently have bucked the trend of declining membership evident elsewhere, but it is failing to attract younger members. The SNP today looks more like an old person's party, albeit little different from other parties in this respect.

A common theme in the elite interviews was the idea that the SNP was not only a political party but also part of the national movement. What was meant by this was that the party was a 'broad church' encompassing all who supported independence and while the party felt itself to be left of centre, it was acknowledged by all those interviewed that it included members with views across the political spectrum. The idea of the SNP as part of the national movement also meant for many senior members that its form was different from that of 'traditional parties' and specifically that it embodied its belief in decentralization and participation. The evidence from this survey suggests that the SNP is more like a conventional political party than some of its senior members realize. On the one hand, this means it is much more coherent ideologically than might have been expected but, on the other, less participative and decentralized than this internal myth would suggest. The old question that has been raised over the years – by those within the SNP, by some of its opponents and by commentators – about what would happen to the party after it achieved its goal of independence looks less relevant. The

SNP is, quite simply, a political party with a range of policies, as coherently articulated and supported as would be found elsewhere. Its structure is far more top-down, especially following reforms instituted since devolution, than the old idea of it being a social movement type organization would suggest.

One of the striking findings has been the extent of agreement between members, activists, and leaders, challenging at least some understandings of the law of curvilinear disparity. However, recent work has offered more subtle interpretations of this law and before we conclude that the SNP provides evidence to undermine it, we should note the context in which this research was conducted. There is nothing like electoral success to breed loyalty to the leadership and unity across a political party, and the membership survey was conducted at the highest point in terms of electoral success in the SNP's history since its foundation. If the SNP did not exhibit the signs of loyalty and unity at this time then it would be in trouble. However, even in more difficult circumstances there is evidence here, given the depth of support for the leadership, to suggest that the SNP leadership would be able to weather internal storms.

Members remain important to political parties. Even as the SNP has been able to attract the kinds of donations that it used to envy (and that its main opponents could take for granted), the main source of income continues to be the ordinary membership. Institutions matter and the restructuring of the SNP, including the introduction of a central membership register, not only benefited academic research (by permitting this study to be conducted) but also ensured that the SNP has a more secure financial base. Members provide the reservoir from which candidates for public office are chosen. The SNP members are particularly actively engaged in campaigning and are essential for a party without corporate support and very little support in the media. The nature of activism is changing with technology. Members who would previously have been limited in what they could do at election time are now able to canvass from their homes using information technology and communications.

While the membership appears content with the structure of the party, there was some disquiet in the elite interviews that the party still had not found a role for its activists in policymaking. The advent of devolution, and thus a large cadre of full-time politicians with publicly funded staff, including Government Ministers after 2007, has altered the power structure within the SNP. This change has occurred not through any formal change in the SNP's constitution but through the opportunities brought about by devolution and a different electoral system. The SNP is far from becoming a cartel party, able to use public resources to maintain its position, but the party now has greater access to state resources than ever before.

Party conference has become less significant, and so in turn have those members who regularly attended, debated, and voted at these annual events and at the regular national councils that met during the year between conferences. Ordinary party members now elect the leader and deputy leader, and choose candidates for the Scottish Parliament and Westminster. The losers in this change have been the party's activists. Though the activists incline to more radical politics, they are not significantly different from the wider membership. The key group of members most likely to cause the leadership any trouble is the large contingent of SNP councillors: active members; holding public office; and more radical than the party as a whole.

The SNP's electoral success is, in part at least, owed to the perception that it has been 'good for Scotland' and likely to form a competent government. The pragmatism involved in this image has overwhelming support. However, a tension will always exist in a party that pursues radical goals: should it moderate its message in appealing for voters or appease members who join in pursuit of more radical objectives? While the members may have endorsed the leadership's pragmatic strategy, the bulk of them joined because they believe in Scottish independence. This objective is what brought them into the party and motivates them to give money and many hours of their time to the party. Managing that balance requires not only leadership but also electoral success and at least some progress towards the key aim. Questions are likely to be raised when a party appears to have stalled in advancing towards its main goal: the goal that brought members into the party. While the SNP appears to be a fairly conventional political party its *raison d'être* remains independence. There may not be another party home for disillusioned members to join but it is conceivable that many might drift away in the event that the party is perceived to have abandoned faith in independence. The increase in membership in recent years includes many members who had left the party. While many may have done so less for reasons of disillusionment than because the party lost contact with them, it is probable that a fair proportion simply regarded it as rational to drift away given the SNP's lack of progress towards its central goal. However, the SNP's constitution lists two primary objectives. The 'furtherance of Scottish interests' is often overlooked in commentaries but many members join the party because they support independence *and* because they see the SNP as 'good for Scotland' or, indeed, only for the latter reason. Defining 'Scottish interests' is open to debate but the SNP seems reasonably united in this respect, interpreting this as requiring a moderate left-wing policy agenda.

The party has long styled itself a civic, as distinct from ethnic, nationalist party. These terms were repeated in almost all elite interviews. These are terms that have become part of the lexicon of SNP politics amongst the party's elite and active membership. It is, however, unlikely that these terms are widely recognized or understood amongst the wider membership. What emerges from the membership survey can be interpreted as endorsement of the SNP as a civic party in terms of its attitudes across a range of policies, attitudes towards national identity and citizenship. The results might equally be interpreted as challenging the value of the civic–ethnic dichotomy. SNP members do not so much endorse a civic identity as endorse a pluralist conception of belonging. In other words, there are many ways of being Scottish, according to SNP members, and these include civic and ethnic definitions of belonging. The conclusion to be drawn from this empirical research is that the value of the distinction lies less in viewing it as a dichotomy, as competing definitions of belonging, but as competing *conceptual* frameworks for viewing identity.

In conclusion, this study offers a snapshot of the SNP at a unique point in its history. It tells us less about the party as it was or as it will be in the future. It is, nonetheless, possible to appreciate the changes that have occurred in the party in recent years. Clearly, the SNP has undergone dramatic change, and this has been largely brought about by its external environment. The party's greatest success in the first seventy years of its history was its survival. It is fitting to conclude by quoting James Halliday, the party's chairman during 1956–60, one of the bleakest periods in its history, who shortly after devolution wrote:

> For good or ill the character of the party has changed for ever as the new century begins. We are now, as a result of our successes, developing as other parties have developed; and will find, as they did that power of initiative and decision will increasingly belong to those of our colleagues who have been elected to something. They are now professionals, and will rapidly acquire skills and general know-how which Parliamentary work involves, and will have the ongoing research and publicity strengths which elevate their expertise far beyond anything that our amateur membership has, until now, been able to provide. (Halliday 2000)

Survey of SNP Members

Please complete this questionnaire and return it as soon as possible, in the pre-paid envelope provided, to Address Data Solutions Ltd, 15 Claverhouse Road, Hillington Park, Glasgow, G52 4RY.

Most questions will require you to put a CROSS (X) in a single box or series of boxes. For example:

Male	
Female	X

Please complete using a blue or black pen and mark your answers as clearly as possible. If there is any question that you would prefer not to answer please just leave it blank and move on to the next. Only you should fill in the questionnaire. All information that you give will be treated with the utmost confidentiality and your anonymity will be respected at all times.

Thank you very much for your help in providing an accurate picture of SNP views at this important time in the party's development.

Any queries about this questionnaire should be addressed to Professor James Mitchell, Chief Investigator. His contact details are below:

Professor James Mitchell
Department of Government
University of Strathclyde
16 Richmond Street
Glasgow G1 1XQ
Tel: 0141 548 2219
e-mail: j.mitchell@strath.ac.uk

Section 1: Your involvement in the SNP

> Q1. In which year did you first join the SNP? PLEASE ENTER THE YEAR IN THE BOXES BELOW

23% of members joined since 2005.

Q2a. Have you been a member continuously since then? PLEASE CROSS ONE BOX	
Yes	81.3
No	18.7

Q2b. When did you LAST rejoin the SNP? PLEASE ENTER THE YEAR IN THE BOXES BELOW

Main point is that 11.3% rejoined since 2005 that is over 50% of the total people that rejoined.

Q3. Thinking back to your first decision to join the party, what were the main reasons that you JOINED the party? PLEASE WRITE IN THE SPACE BELOW

Q4. How active do you consider yourself to be in the SNP right now? PLEASE CROSS ONE BOX	
Very active	11.6
Fairly active	21.3
Not very active	39.8
Not at all active	27.2

Q5. How often do you normally attend local SNP meetings? PLEASE CROSS ONE BOX	
Every month	19.4
Every few months	15.0
About once a year	12.6
Less often than that	16.7
Never	36.3

Q6. How much time do you devote to party activities on average each <u>month</u>?
PLEASE CROSS ONE BOX

None	56.6
1–2 hours	21.4
2–5 hours	9.9
5–10 hours	5.6
10–20 hours	2.9
20–40 hours	1.5
More than 40 hours	2.0

Q7. For this question we'd like you to estimate the <u>total</u> financial contribution that you make <u>each year</u> (including membership fees, contributions to fundraising initiatives, standing orders, etc.) to a) the local party; and b) headquarters. PLEASE WRITE IN THE AMOUNTS BELOW

To the local party	£40
To Headquarters	£44

Q8. Now we would like to ask you about political activities in which you may have taken part on behalf of the SNP. Thinking of the <u>last five years</u>, how often have you done the following? PLEASE CROSS ONE BOX IN EACH ROW

	Very often	Fairly often	Not very often	Not at all
Displayed an election poster	40.6	18.7	13.3	27.4
Stood for office in the party	8.6	5.0	5.8	80.5
Attended a national party conference	12.2	8.8	13.6	65.3
Delivered leaflets *during* an election	32.4	13.8	13.1	40.7
Delivered leaflets *between* elections	17.2	11.3	15.8	55.7
Helped at a party function (e.g. social event, jumble sale) or with fundraising	16.7	14.8	19.6	48.9
Attended a party meeting	21.4	13.9	28.6	36.2
Canvassed voters door-to-door	13.4	9.2	13.6	63.8
Canvassed voters by telephone	5.4	4.9	10.3	79.3

Q9a. Have you ever been a candidate for the SNP in a local or national election?
PLEASE CROSS ONE BOX

Yes	18.0
No	82.0

Q9b. Could you indicate in which type(s) of election you were a candidate?
PLEASE CROSS AS MANY BOXES AS APPLY

For local government	16.6
For the Scottish Parliament	1.6
For the UK Parliament	2.5
For the European Parliament	0.4

Q10. Have you ever held any of the following positions or offices within/for the party? PLEASE CROSS AS MANY BOXES AS APPLY OR CHOOSE 'NONE'

Branch office-bearer (e.g. convener, secretary, treasurer)	29.6
Constituency office-bearer (e.g. convener, secretary, treasurer)	14.1
Member of National Executive Committee	1.9
Member of National Council	3.2
Councillor	5.0
MSP	0.6
MP	0.4
MEP	0.3
None	44.9

Q11. Are you currently a member of any of the following groups within the party? PLEASE CROSS AS MANY BOXES AS APPLY OR CHOOSE 'NONE'

Federation of Student Nationalists	0.8
SNP Trade Union Group (SNP-TUG)	1.3
Young Scots for Independence (YSI)	0.9
Scots Asians for Independence	0.2
Business for Independence	0.8
None	96.0

Q12a. How often, if at all, have you accessed the party's headquarters website in the last twelve months? PLEASE CROSS ONE BOX

At least once a week	7.3
Around once a month	19.6
Not as often as that	33.9
Never/I don't have web access	39.2

Q12b. Have you accessed the 'members only' section on the party's website? PLEASE CROSS ONE BOX

Yes	28.9
No	46.5
No access	24.5

Section 2: Your other political interests

Q13. Please look at the following list of voluntary organizations. Are you now or have you in the past been a member of any of these organizations, either in Scotland or as a UK member? PLEASE CROSS AS MANY BOXES AS APPLY

	Now	Not now but in the past
Trade union	18.5	37.9
Church or religious group	22.5	19.5
School Board/Parent-Teacher Association	3.3	16.2
A group helping the elderly or disabled (e.g. Help the Aged)	7.5	10.3
Arts, music or cultural group	15.9	13.4
Local community action group (e.g. on housing)	7.8	11.5
Third world development organization (e.g. Action Aid)	7.2	5.4
Conservation group (e.g. National Trust)	18.1	10.9
Professional association	20.9	17.6
Youth work (e.g. scouts, guides, youth club)	5.2	24.2
Sports club or recreation group	16.4	17.9
Women's group	3.7	6.8
Peace movement group (e.g. CND)	4.5	8.8
Human Rights Group (e.g. Amnesty International)	6.2	6.2
Environmental Group (e.g. Friends of the Earth)	6.9	6.0
Other (please specify: _____)	12.2	0.2

Q14a. Have you ever been a member of another political party? PLEASE CROSS ONE BOX

Yes	13.5
No	86.5

Q14b. Which party or parties were you a member of? PLEASE CROSS AS MANY BOXES AS APPLY

Conservative	3.0
Labour	6.5
Liberal Democrat	1.7
Green	0.4
Scottish Socialist Party/Solidarity	0.6
Plaid Cymru	0.4
Other (please specify: _____)	2.3

Section 3: Your views on political issues

Q15. How much do you agree or disagree with each of the following statements? PLEASE CROSS ONE BOX IN EACH ROW

	Strongly agree	Agree	Neither agree nor disagree	Disagree	Strongly disagree
People who break the law should be given stiffer sentences	33.2	29.6	26.9	8.8	1.4
Working people get their fair share of the nation's wealth	10.7	16.5	16.7	40.2	16.0
We worry too much about the environment and not enough about prices and jobs	6.2	19.9	25.6	36.0	12.3
There is one law for the rich and one law for the poor	25.4	40.5	18.8	12.3	3.0
Young people today don't have enough respect for traditional values	26.1	37.4	21.5	12.8	2.2
Private enterprise is the best way to solve Britain's economic problems	7.1	21.5	38.0	25.5	7.9
The European Union has become too centralized	24.3	35.5	23.7	14.1	2.4
We criticize our nation of Scotland too much.	32.4	39.3	14.7	11.2	2.5

Q16. Here are various options for governing Scotland. Could you rank the top three in your order of preference: that is, put 1 by your first preference, 2 by your second preference, and 3 by your third preference? PLEASE USE NUMBERS TO INDICATE RANKINGS

	1	2	3	None
The Scottish Parliament should be abolished and all Scottish laws passed by Westminster again	0.3	0.2	1.3	98.2
There should be no change to the present arrangements: Scotland should have a devolved Parliament with limited powers	0.7	1.1	11.7	86.5
The Scottish Parliament's powers should be increased and it should raise more of its own taxes	10.9	30.1	43.6	15.4
Scotland should be independent within the European Union	56.9	21.8	4.9	16.4
Scotland should be independent outside the European Union	19.2	32.4	19.0	29.5

Q17. Thinking about matters for which Westminster is fully or partly responsible, which if any of the following do you think should become completely the responsibility of the Scottish Parliament? Could you rank the top three in your order of preference: that is, put 1 by the matter that you would most like to see under Scottish Parliament control, and so on? PLEASE USE NUMBERS TO INDICATE RANKINGS

	1st	2nd	3rd	None
Defence & Foreign Affairs	12.5	14.0	12.0	61.4
Social Security & Pensions	7.2	14.0	11.3	67.4
Trade & Currency	5.1	11.8	11.0	72.2
Abortion and embryo research	1.9	0.6	1.0	96.6
Economic policy & Taxation	52.1	13.6	8.0	26.3
Energy	6.7	14.7	11.2	67.4
European Affairs	2.8	5.4	6.6	85.2
Civil service	1.9	3.0	4.4	90.7
Broadcasting	5.2	6.2	12.4	76.3
Immigration & extradition	4.7	5.6	8.3	81.4
Transport policy	2.3	4.1	6.2	87.5

Q18. Here are some more statements. How much do you agree or disagree with each one? PLEASE CROSS ONE BOX IN EACH ROW

	Strongly agree	Agree	Neither agree nor disagree	Disagree	Strongly disagree
Government should redistribute income from the better off to the less well off	20.0	43.6	22.1	12.1	2.1
The monarchy has no place in a modern democracy	35.2	21.8	23.3	14.3	5.5
The death penalty is never justified, even for very serious crimes	28.1	23.4	10.9	24.0	13.6
High income tax makes people less willing to work hard	12.4	32.3	22.9	28.8	3.7
Separate Catholic schools should be phased out	36.0	28.4	17.6	10.7	7.3
For the sake of the environment, car users should pay higher taxes	7.3	24.3	22.2	33.1	13.0
Homosexual relations are always wrong	10.3	10.7	26.5	25.1	27.5
Everyone's taxes should go up to provide better old age pensions for all	12.5	41.0	27.3	16.3	2.8
Membership of NATO is in Scotland's strategic interest	13.5	39.2	24.3	14.7	8.2

Q19. In politics people sometimes talk of 'left' and 'right'. Using the following scale, where 0 means left and 10 means right, what number do you think best describes the positions of the following parties? What about the position of Alex Salmond? Finally, what about yourself?

	Left										Right	
	0	1	2	3	4	5	6	7	8	9	10	Don't know
Conservatives	1.0	0.2	0.5	0.7	0.9	2.7	5.9	16.7	30.9	15.2	21.7	3.6
Labour	4.4	1.9	3.6	5.6	7.7	11.6	14.6	18.2	15.3	7.3	5.9	3.9
Liberal Democrats	1.2	0.5	1.4	4.6	11.6	25.8	20.4	14.3	7.5	2.4	1.2	9.2
SNP	1.2	0.7	4.2	13.7	28.7	31.5	10.7	3.1	1.1	0.5	1.8	2.8
Green Party	2.2	3.5	9.8	17.3	19.5	18.8	7.0	3.8	2.2	0.9	0.9	14.3
Alex Salmond	1.4	1.1	4.2	12.0	23.7	31.8	13.2	4.3	1.7	0.7	2.1	4.0
Yourself	3.7	3.8	8.3	14.1	17.8	24.3	11.2	6.6	3.8	1.3	2.1	3.0

Q20. Here are some more statements. How much do you agree or disagree with each one? PLEASE CROSS ONE BOX IN EACH ROW

	Strongly agree	Agree	Neither agree nor disagree	Disagree	Strongly disagree
Censorship of films and magazines have no place in a free society	13.9	24.8	15.7	37.9	7.7
It is not government's responsibility to provide a job for everyone who wants one	7.6	39.0	18.8	28.9	5.7
In principle, identity cards are a good idea	8.2	26.0	11.4	20.6	33.7
Management will always try to get the better of employees if it gets the chance	13.8	39.8	22.8	20.1	3.5
The government should reduce spending on public services in order to cut taxes	3.4	9.5	16.1	52.4	18.7
The law should always be obeyed, even if a particular law is wrong	6.6	28.6	21.4	36.1	7.2
Private fee-paying education should have its charitable status removed	26.5	38.4	17.4	13.0	4.7
Nuclear energy is essential for future prosperity	6.1	13.5	16.6	31.1	32.7
It is better for a country if everyone shares the same customs and traditions	9.8	19.3	21.4	37.4	12.2

Section 4: Your identity

Q21. People differ in how they think of or describe themselves. Which in the following list are most important to you in describing who you are? Please rank the top three most important to you, marking 1 by the most important and so on? PLEASE USE NUMBERS TO INDICATE RANKINGS	1st	2nd	3rd	None
Your social class	2.3	5.3	6.7	85.7
Your national identity	59.9	14.4	7.2	18.5
Your age group/generation	5.6	13.5	13.3	67.6
Your gender	5.4	7.5	6.5	80.5
Your religion	4.6	6.0	5.1	84.3
The place (village or town) where you live	3.8	14.8	13.8	67.7
Your ethnic group	1.0	2.5	3.0	93.5
The job that you do (or did)	6.6	12.9	16.4	64.1
Your political allegiances	2.4	14.2	16.2	67.1
Other (please specify: _____)	2.8	1.2	2.0	94.1

Q22. Who we are and where we live may be expressed in terms of our Home Street, Area, Town, County, Nation, State, Europe, The World. Thinking in this way about where you live now, which of the options below are the most important to you generally in your everyday life? Please rank the top three, marking 1 by the most important and so on. PLEASE USE NUMBERS TO INDICATE RANKINGS	1st	2nd	3rd	None
The street in which you live	5.0	4.1	6.7	84.2
The local area or district	10.1	17.3	17.3	55.2
The town or city	8.2	21.9	14.7	55.1
The county or region (e.g. Lothian, Lanarkshire, Western Isles)	5.0	18.6	11.4	64.9
The nation in which you live	60.1	13.6	9.4	17.0
The United Kingdom	1.1	2.4	3.9	92.6
Europe	1.0	9.8	14.0	75.3
The world	2.9	3.6	11.7	81.8
Other (please specify: _____)	1.0	0.4	0.5	98.1
None of these	0.3	0.0	0.3	99.4

Q23. Which if any of the following <u>best</u> describes how you see yourself? CROSS ONE BOX

Scottish not British	77.4
More Scottish than British	16.0
Equally Scottish and British	2.6
More British than Scottish	0.2
British not Scottish	0.3
Other (please specify: _____)	3.5

Q24. Being Scottish has lots of different aspects, some of which are listed below. Which, if any, of these is important to you personally when you think about being Scottish? Please rank the top three, marking 1 by the most important and so on. PLEASE USE NUMBERS TO INDICATE RANKINGS, OR CHOOSE 'NONE'

	1st	2nd	3rd	None
The Scottish countryside and scenery	10.3	14.1	16.6	59.0
The Scottish legal system	2.0	4.0	5.3	88.7
The Scottish people	40.8	15.8	9.9	33.5
Scottish history	12.7	17.9	14.1	55.2
Scottish sporting achievements	1.0	1.6	2.9	94.5
The Scottish Parliament	11.6	11.5	11.5	65.4
Scottish art, music and literature	3.3	6.5	9.9	80.3
Scottish education and science	3.9	10.2	10.7	75.2
Scotland's democratic tradition	9.5	10.4	10.3	69.8
Other (please specify: _____)	1.0	0.4	0.5	98.1
None			0.1	99.9

Q25. There are also aspects of life in Scotland that make some Scots less proud of their country. Some of these are listed below. Do any of them make you less proud of Scotland? If so, please again rank the top three, marking 1 by the aspect that makes you least proud, and so on. PLEASE USE NUMBERS TO INDICATE RANKINGS, OR CHOOSE 'NONE'

	1st	2nd	3rd	None
Poverty	15.1	15.1	14.4	55.3
Lack of self-confidence as a nation	32.2	10.2	6.9	50.7
Sectarianism	16.7	17.3	14.6	51.4
European Union policies	11.1	7.0	6.5	75.4
Alcohol and drug problems	11.3	17.1	15.9	55.6
Image associated with tartan	0.6	1.7	2.4	95.3
A 'chip on the shoulder' regarding England	2.6	6.4	7.2	83.8
Poor health record	5.7	13.9	17.0	63.4
Being too concerned with the past	0.6	1.9	3.8	93.6
Other (please specify: _____)	0.8	0.6	0.9	97.8
None			0.3	99.7

Q26. Overall, how proud would you say you feel about being Scottish? PLEASE CROSS ONE BOX

Very proud	82.5
Fairly proud	14.9
Not very proud	1.4
Not at all proud	0.4
Don't feel Scottish	0.8

Q27. Here are three statements about being Scottish. Please indicate how much you agree or disagree with each one. PLEASE CROSS ONE BOX IN EACH ROW

	Strongly agree	Agree	Neither agree nor disagree	Disagree	Strongly disagree
You can be equally proud of being British and of being Scottish; it's not a matter of choosing between them	4.6	13.9	12.7	34.6	34.2
Sometimes it is more appropriate to say you are British and sometimes it is more appropriate to say you are Scottish	4.1	16.4	10.8	31.8	36.8
When someone criticizes Scotland, it feels like a personal insult	31.0	38.6	14.8	12.4	3.1

Q28. Thinking about Scottish society, please rate each of the following on a scale from 0 to 10, where 0 means 'very poor' and 10 means 'very good'. PLEASE CROSS ONE BOX IN EACH ROW

	0	1	2	3	4	5	6	7	8	9	10	Don't know
Education	0.6	0.3	0.9	2.4	4.2	9.4	13.2	24.8	29.9	7.6	5.6	1.1
Environmental quality	0.4	0.5	1.0	2.4	5.4	12.1	14.3	22.8	25.2	10.0	4.4	1.5
Housing conditions	1.5	1.6	4.8	11.9	20.2	24.9	17.4	10.5	3.8	0.8	0.8	1.7
The state of the economy	1.0	1.1	3.2	8.4	13.4	22.7	20.9	15.6	8.2	1.6	1.1	2.9
The nation's health	3.1	5.1	14.1	22.8	21.6	16.9	8.1	4.1	1.6	0.7	1.0	0.9

Q29. Over the years, there has been talk of many different potential threats to the Scottish nation. Several of these are listed below. Which do you think <u>are</u> or <u>were</u> particularly important threats? Please rank the three most important, marking 1 by the most important and so on. PLEASE USE NUMBERS TO INDICATE RANKINGS

	1st	2nd	3rd	None
Thatcherism	11.0	7.1	6.6	75.3
Lack of self-confidence as a nation	23.3	10.7	11.0	55.0
Immigration from England	2.0	2.5	2.9	92.6
European Union policies	1.9	3.6	3.4	91.0
Being denied North Sea oil revenues	23.9	20.5	14.3	41.3
Immigration from outside the UK	2.4	2.9	2.6	92.0
Nuclear weapons	6.4	10.0	8.6	75.0
Emigration	2.3	4.1	4.7	88.8
London Government	17.2	16.3	15.5	51.0
Mass media	1.7	4.8	7.1	86.4
English nationalism	0.6	1.0	1.7	96.7
Nuclear waste	2.8	5.0	6.7	85.5
Foreign ownership of Scottish businesses	2.6	5.2	7.8	84.4

Q30. Some people say the following things are important for being truly Scottish. Others say they are not important. How important do you think each of the following is? PLEASE CROSS ONE BOX IN EACH ROW

	Very	Fairly	Not very	Not at all
To have Scottish ancestry	24.4	31.9	26.8	16.9
To have been born in Scotland	33.0	29.7	22.3	15.1
To live in Scotland now	47.5	31.8	14.5	6.2
To have lived in Scotland for most of one's life	28.1	37.4	25.7	8.8
To be a Christian	12.1	12.5	19.1	56.2
To respect Scottish political institutions and laws	59.2	33.5	5.5	1.8
To feel Scottish	77.9	18.3	2.7	1.0
To be able to speak English, Gaelic, or Scots	38.5	34.0	17.4	10.1

Section 5: Your views on the SNP

Q31. Please indicate how much you agree or disagree with these statements. PLEASE CROSS ONE BOX IN EACH ROW					
	Strongly agree	Agree	Neither agree nor disagree	Disagree	Strongly disagree
The SNP's primary goal is independence and all else should be secondary	38.4	32.7	11.0	16.4	1.5
To achieve the ultimate goal of independence, the SNP should concentrate on making devolution work	35.7	50.1	9.3	4.1	0.7
To achieve independence the SNP must be prepared to work with other parties and organizations	29.7	60.1	7.5	2.4	0.3
The SNP's primary goal is independence but this may need to take second place when other matters arise affecting Scotland	13.9	50.8	15.0	16.1	4.2
The creation of a Scottish Parliament with devolved powers makes independence more difficult to achieve for the SNP	3.9	12.3	16.1	50.2	17.6
Participating in a governing coalition in the Scottish Parliament would involve the SNP compromising on its goal of independence	6.6	26.2	23.4	35.7	8.1

Q32. Thinking about the SNP's future direction, how much do you agree or disagree with these statements? PLEASE CROSS ONE BOX IN EACH ROW

	Strongly agree	Agree	Neither agree nor disagree	Disagree	Strongly disagree
The SNP should always stand by its principles even if this loses votes	30.1	50.7	11.8	6.6	0.7
The SNP should put effort into exploring pacts with other parties, even if this involves policy compromises	4.3	43.0	26.4	23.4	3.0
The SNP should put emphasis on social issues and representing the under-privileged in society, rather than promoting itself as a business-friendly party	11.0	28.5	37.5	20.7	2.4
The SNP should spend less time on creating a professional media image, and put more effort into promoting its programme and policies	10.6	30.1	34.7	21.9	2.7

Q33. Next, here are some statements on politics and party members. Please indicate how much you agree or disagree with each of these. PLEASE CROSS ONE BOX IN EACH ROW

	Strongly agree	Agree	Neither agree nor disagree	Disagree	Strongly disagree
People like me can have a real influence on politics if they are prepared to get involved	21.6	56.7	15.9	5.2	0.6
A person like me could do a good job of being a local SNP councillor	13.4	32.5	28.5	20.7	4.8
Being an active party member is a good way to meet interesting people	11.9	55.0	29.4	3.2	0.6
Party activists, of all parties, tend to be extremists	1.7	8.8	20.3	53.2	15.9
When SNP members are united and work together they can really change Scotland	44.9	50.5	4.0	0.4	0.3
The local party has really made a difference to our local community	12.3	36.9	40.0	9.4	1.4
Party members lack the knowledge necessary to make policy	2.0	10.5	28.9	45.6	13.1

Q34. Next, here are some statements on politics and party members. Please indicate how much you agree or disagree with each of these. PLEASE CROSS ONE BOX IN EACH ROW

	Strongly agree	Agree	Neither agree nor disagree	Disagree	Strongly disagree
By and large SNP politicians try to represent the views of ordinary party members	19.1	67.6	10.8	2.3	0.1
The only time SNP members hear from the party is when they want some money	2.0	10.9	19.8	55.4	11.9
Ordinary party members do not have enough say in determining SNP policy	2.8	14.8	36.2	41.2	5.0
The party does not do enough to ensure that equal numbers of men and women are selected as SNP election candidates	1.4	4.4	40.7	42.3	11.1
The SNP leadership has too much influence over the selection of local candidates for elections	1.8	5.8	42.8	41.7	7.9
It is right that SNP members who attend party meetings and conferences have more say in the party than those who are never active	11.0	56.9	15.4	14.4	2.3
SNP members have a right to be consulted in any coalition talks between the SNP and other parties	14.1	44.3	23.7	16.1	1.7

Q35. Please think about your general impressions of the SNP, and describe them using the following scales from 0 to 10. For example, on the first scale, if you think the party is very moderate, you would tick a box towards the right-hand side; if you think the party is very extreme, you would tick a box on the left. PLEASE CROSS ONE BOX IN EACH ROW

	0	1	2	3	4	5	6	7	8	9	10	
Extreme	0.7	0.3	0.9	2.3	5.9	18.8	10.4	16.6	21.9	9.2	12.9	Moderate
Badly run	0.9	0.7	1.0	1.1	1.3	4.3	5.3	15.3	30.3	21.4	18.2	Well run
Divided	1.1	1.1	1.7	1.7	2.1	6.8	7.2	16.2	27.0	18.8	16.4	United
Good for one class	1.4	0.7	1.2	1.2	1.1	6.4	4.4	12.4	25.3	19.2	26.7	Good for all classes
Not capable of strong government	1.5	0.7	0.5	0.5	0.6	1.7	1.8	5.7	18.1	25.9	42.9	Capable of strong government
Radical	1.9	1.8	6.6	12.3	15.0	26.9	12.8	9.5	7.3	3.1	2.7	Conservative
Working class	1.2	0.4	1.3	3.3	8.4	50.0	17.6	9.2	4.3	1.7	2.6	Middle class

Q36. Now please think about your general impressions of ALEX SALMOND, and describe him using the same type of scale. PLEASE CROSS ONE BOX IN EACH ROW

	0	1	2	3	4	5	6	7	8	9	10	
Uncaring	0.5	0.4	0.4	0.5	0.6	3.1	5.8	12.9	24.7	18.8	32.4	Caring
Weak leader	1.1	0.3	0.3	0.1	0.2	0.4	0.8	3.4	12.0	23.8	57.6	Strong leader
Dislikeable	1.0	0.6	0.7	0.5	0.8	2.6	3.8	9.0	19.3	22.6	39.2	Likeable
Indecisive	0.9	0.5	0.2	0.2	0.2	0.8	1.3	4.4	16.7	26.4	48.5	Decisive
Untrustworthy	1.3	0.4	0.3	0.3	0.7	2.0	2.6	6.7	17.1	23.6	45.0	Trustworthy

Q37. Thinking now about how the SNP is organized, do you think these party institutions and individuals have too little, too much or the right amount of power in the party. Use the following scale, where 0 means 'far too little power', 5 means 'the right amount of power' and 10 means 'far too much power'. PLEASE CROSS ONE BOX IN EACH ROW

	Far too little power				Right amount					Far too much power		
	0	1	2	3	4	5	6	7	8	9	10	Don't know
Party leader	1.2	0.4	0.7	1.1	2.9	59.3	15.3	6.8	4.2	1.2	0.7	6.3
Deputy leader	0.9	0.4	0.6	1.6	4.4	61.8	13.1	4.8	2.6	1.1	0.4	8.2
MSPs	1.1	0.7	1.4	3.3	8.9	56.3	11.2	4.1	2.2	0.6	0.3	9.7
MPs	2.1	1.6	2.8	5.1	8.5	47.5	9.7	4.1	3.4	1.9	1.6	11.7
Staff at party HQ	0.6	0.3	0.9	1.7	4.5	47.3	9.1	4.8	2.4	1.0	0.6	26.7
National Executive Committee	0.6	0.4	0.6	1.9	5.0	46.1	11.0	5.4	2.7	0.8	0.4	25.1
National Conference/ National Council	0.7	0.5	0.9	3.0	7.7	46.3	9.5	3.8	2.0	0.6	0.4	24.5
National Assembly	0.9	0.6	1.3	3.2	6.4	45.8	8.3	3.2	1.9	0.5	0.5	27.3
Standing Orders & Agenda Committee	0.6	0.4	0.7	2.0	5.1	41.1	8.8	5.1	3.5	1.8	0.9	30.1
Constituency Assocns/local branches	1.6	1.3	3.2	8.9	13.7	42.2	6.1	1.9	1.1	0.4	0.3	19.4
Ordinary members	3.3	3.3	5.9	10.8	14.2	43.1	4.5	0.9	0.5	0.2	0.2	13.1

Q38. Here is another 0 to 10 scale, where this time 0 means 'strongly dislike' and 10 means 'strongly like'. Using this scale, please tell us how you feel about the following parties. PLEASE CROSS ONE BOX IN EACH ROW

	Strongly dislike										Strongly like	
	0	1	2	3	4	5	6	7	8	9	10	Don't know
SNP	0.2	0.1	0.1	0.1	0.1	0.3	0.7	2.1	9.5	15.7	71.2	0.1
Labour	35.7	10.1	14.8	12.7	9.4	9.5	4.0	2.3	0.8	0.2	0.2	0.4
Conservatives	29.0	11.6	16.1	13.9	10.3	10.6	4.5	2.2	0.9	0.3	0.2	0.4
Liberal Democrats	23.4	10.6	13.6	13.5	12.1	14.5	6.0	3.5	1.5	0.3	0.1	1.0
Greens	5.8	3.1	5.4	6.9	9.4	20.4	13.3	13.5	11.9	4.5	2.8	2.9
Plaid Cymru	2.4	0.7	0.9	1.1	1.8	8.3	5.7	10.1	16.9	13.5	18.7	19.9

Q39. Now, using the same scale, please tell us how you feel about the following politicians. PLEASE CROSS ONE BOX IN EACH ROW

	Strongly dislike										Strongly like	
	0	1	2	3	4	5	6	7	8	9	10	Don't know
Alex Salmond	0.2	0.2	0.2	0.2	0.2	0.7	1.4	3.7	13.0	20.2	59.9	0.2
Nicola Sturgeon	0.3	0.2	0.3	0.5	0.9	1.8	3.7	8.0	17.3	21.2	44.9	0.9
John Swinney	0.2	0.2	0.3	0.6	0.7	3.0	5.1	10.5	20.3	21.4	35.4	2.3
Fiona Hyslop	0.3	0.2	0.3	0.6	1.2	5.9	7.4	13.8	21.3	15.9	18.0	15.0
Kenny Macaskill	0.3	0.4	0.6	0.9	1.8	5.2	6.4	13.7	19.6	18.9	22.3	9.9
Richard Lochhead	0.3	0.2	0.3	0.8	1.5	6.1	7.0	11.3	16.0	13.9	17.2	25.2
Angus Robertson	0.3	0.2	0.3	0.7	1.2	5.8	6.4	11.0	16.4	14.1	18.2	25.4
Alex Neil	0.7	0.5	0.9	1.4	2.4	7.2	7.5	12.2	16.6	15.0	17.1	18.6
Michael Russell	0.7	0.6	1.0	1.5	2.3	7.1	8.2	12.0	17.5	14.7	15.1	19.3
Roseanna Cunningham	0.8	0.7	1.3	1.6	3.3	7.2	8.5	13.7	18.5	16.8	18.8	8.7
Angus MacNeil	0.4	0.2	0.5	0.8	1.6	6.3	7.2	10.7	15.4	13.6	18.4	24.8
Winnie Ewing	0.9	0.5	0.8	0.9	1.3	3.9	4.5	7.6	14.3	18.5	42.0	4.8
Wendy Alexander	41.2	14.6	13.8	9.2	6.0	5.6	2.3	1.5	1.3	0.8	1.1	2.6
Annabel Goldie	10.9	7.7	11.4	12.5	12.8	16.3	8.7	7.1	5.4	2.0	1.7	3.5
Nicol Stephen	29.1	14.3	13.9	11.7	8.6	7.7	2.9	2.2	1.3	0.4	0.5	7.3
Gordon Brown	37.9	12.5	12.4	9.7	7.9	8.4	4.1	2.6	1.9	0.9	0.8	1.0
David Cameron	26.8	14.7	15.6	13.4	9.7	9.4	3.7	2.5	1.7	0.6	0.5	1.4
Margo MacDonald	4.5	2.7	3.5	4.6	6.4	13.8	9.6	11.4	14.3	11.2	14.4	3.7

Section 6: About yourself

Q40. Are you:	
Male	68.2
Female	31.8

Q41. In which year were you born? PLEASE ENTER IN THE BOXES BELOW

Average year of birth 1949.

Q42. Which of the following best describes your current employment status? PLEASE CROSS ONE BOX

Employed full-time (30 hours or more a week)	32.0
Employed part-time (less than 30 hours a week)	6.0
Self-employed	10.0
Looking after the home full-time	2.3
In full-time education	2.4
Retired from work	39.4
Permanently sick or disabled	4.4
Unemployed	1.4
Other (please specify: _____)	2.0

The following set of questions is about your occupation. If you are not in a job at the moment, please answer the questions with reference to your last job. If you've never had a job, please go to Q49.

Q43. Do you work as an employee or are you self-employed? PLEASE CROSS ONE BOX

Employee	78.9
Self-employed with employees	8.9
Self-employed/freelance without employees	12.1

Q44a. Please indicate below how many people work for your employer at the place where you work, and then go to Q45. PLEASE CROSS ONE BOX
Q44b. Please indicate below how many people you employ, and then go to Q46. PLEASE CROSS ONE BOX

1 to 24 people	32.3
25 or more people	67.7

Q45. Do you supervise any other employees on a day-to-day basis? CROSS ONE BOX

Yes	50.2
No	49.8

Q46. Which of these best describes the sort of work you do/did? CROSS ONE BOX

Modern professional occupations (e.g. teacher, nurse, physiotherapist, social worker, welfare officer, artist, musician, police officer (sergeant or above), software designer)	32.5
Clerical and intermediate occupations (e.g. secretary, personal assistant, clerical worker, office clerk, call centre agent, nursing auxiliary, nursery nurse)	12.4
Senior managers or administrators (usually responsible for planning, organizing and coordinating work and for finance, e.g. finance manager, chief executive)	13.0
Technical and craft occupations (e.g. motor mechanic, fitter, inspector, plumber, printer, tool maker, electrician, gardener, train driver)	9.7
Semi-routine manual and service occupations (e.g. postal worker, machine operative, security guard, caretaker, farm worker, catering assistant, receptionist, sales assistant)	6.5
Routine manual and service occupations (e.g. HGV driver, van driver, cleaner, porter, packer, sewing machinist, messenger, labourer, waiter/waitress, bar staff)	5.3
Middle or junior managers (e.g. office manager, retail manager, bank manager, restaurant manager, warehouse manager – publican)	7.2
Traditional professional occupations (e.g. accountant, solicitor, medical practitioner, scientist, civil/mechanical engineer)	13.4

Q47. In which sector of the economy do/did you work? PLEASE CROSS ONE BOX	
Agriculture, fishing, hunting, forestry	3.4
Industry (e.g. manufacturing, mining, construction, utilities)	17.2
Education	17.7
Health, social services	12.6
Media (newspaper, radio, TV), culture (film, theatre)	2.3
Security services (e.g. police, armed forces, etc.)	2.4
Other public administration (e.g. local authority, civil service)	13.8
Banking, finance, insurance, property	18.1
Other services (e.g. retail trade, transport, catering, leisure, cleaning, etc.) Other (please specify: _____)	12.6

Q48. For which type of organization do/did you work? PLEASE CROSS ONE BOX	
Private sector firm or company	46.3
Public sector employer	48.2
Charity/voluntary sector (charitable company, churches, interest groups etc.)	5.4
Other (please specify: _____)	

Q49. Which of the following categories represents the total annual income of your household (from all sources, before tax)? PLEASE CROSS ONE BOX	
Under £10,000	13.0
£10,000–£19,999	23.6
£20,000–£29,999	20.1
£30,000–£39,999	14.4
£40,000–£49,999	8.8
£50,000–£59,999	6.6
£60,000–£79,999	6.6
£80,000–£99,999	3.1
Over £100,000	3.9

Q50. How old were you when you completed full-time education? CROSS ONE BOX	
15 or under	25.7
16	17.4
17	9.5
18	6.8
19 or over	38.0
Still in full-time education	2.5

Q51. Which of these is your highest educational qualification? PLEASE CROSS ONE BOX	
None	12.5
'Standard' Grade/'O' Grade/'O' Level/GCSE	13.4
Higher/'A' Level	9.7
Professional/Vocational qualification	16.3
HNC, HND	8.7
University or old Polytechnic degree (e.g. BA, BSc)	22.8
Postgraduate degree	12.5
Other (please specify: _____)	4.2

Q53a. Do you ever think of yourself as belonging to a social class? CROSS ONE BOX	
Yes	42.7
No	57.3

Q53b. If you had to choose, which of these best describes you now? CROSS ONE BOX	
Working class	38.1
Middle class	44.3
Other (please specify: _____)	–
Cannot choose	17.7

Q53c. And which of these best describes your parents' social class when you were born? PLEASE CROSS ONE BOX

Working class	68.5
Middle class	25.7
Other (please specify: _____)	–
Cannot choose	5.8

Q54a. Do you regard yourself as belonging to any particular religion? CROSS ONE BOX

Yes	57.4
No	42.6

Q54b. Which denomination is that? PLEASE CROSS ONE BOX

Roman Catholic Church	17.5
Church of Scotland	64.5
Other Presbyterian	3.1
Church of England/Wales	1.4
Episcopalian	3.0
Methodist	0.6
Other Christian	3.8
Muslim	0.3
Hindu	0.1
Jewish	0.3
Other (please specify: _____)	5.4

Q54c. Apart from such special occasions as weddings, funerals and baptisms and so on, nowadays, how often do you attend services or meetings connected with your religion? PLEASE CROSS ONE BOX

Once a week or more	22.5
At least once in two weeks	6.9
At least once a month	8.3
At least twice a year	11.7
At least once a year	6.8
Never or practically never	37.5
Varies too much to say	6.4

Q54d. How religious do you consider yourself to be? PLEASE CROSS ONE BOX	
Very religious	10.7
Fairly religious	41.4
Not very religious	30.0
Not at all religious	17.8

Q55. Please indicate your ethnic origins. PLEASE CROSS ONE BOX	
Black: of African origin	0.1
Black: of Caribbean origin	0.0
Black: of other origin	0.1
Asian: of Indian origin	0.1
Asian: of Pakistani origin	0.1
Asian: of Bangladeshi origin	0.0
Asian: of Chinese origin	0.0
Asian: of other origin	0.4
White: of any European origin	89.3
White: of other origin	3.3
Mixed origin	0.4
Other (please specify: _____)	6.2

Q56. In what country were you born? PLEASE CROSS ONE BOX	
Scotland	89.4
England	6.7
Wales	0.4
N. Ireland	0.3
Republic of Ireland	0.3
Other (please specify: _____)	2.9

Q57. And in what country were each of your parents born? PLEASE CROSS ONE BOX IN EACH COLUMN

	Mother	Father
Scotland	89.1	86.1
England	7.8	7.1
Wales	0.6	0.6
N. Ireland	1.1	0.9
Republic of Ireland	1.3	1.2
Other (please specify: _____)	0.0	4.1

Q58a. Have you ever lived outside Scotland for a period of six months or longer? PLEASE CROSS ONE BOX

Yes	51.0
No	49.0

Q58b. Where was that? PLEASE CROSS ONE BOX

Scotland	3.9
England	47.2
Wales	1.2
N. Ireland	1.3
Republic of Ireland	1.6
Other (please specify: _____)	44.9

Q59. What is your marital status? PLEASE CROSS ONE BOX

Married	61.5
In a civil partnership	0.7
Widowed	8.5
Divorced/separated	8.3
Living with partner	6.5
Single	14.4
Living without a partner	0.4

Q60a. How often do you read a daily morning newspaper? PLEASE CROSS ONE BOX	
Every day	62.6
Fairly often	18.6
Not very often	12.1
Not at all	6.8

Q60b. Which daily morning newspaper do you read most often? CROSS ONE BOX	
Scottish Daily Express	3.7
Scottish Daily Mail	8.0
Scottish Daily Mirror	0.8
Daily Star	0.8
Scottish Sun	5.5
Daily Record	7.2
Daily Telegraph	1.2
Financial Times	0.7
Guardian	2.7
Independent	1.7
Times	2.3
Scotsman	15.1
(Glasgow) Herald	33.8
(Aberdeen) Press and Journal	8.3
Courier/Dundee Courier	5.6
Paisley Daily Express	0.2
Other (please specify: _____)	2.7

Q61. Do you have any children in your care aged 15 or younger? If so, how many? Are any of these children under 5? PLEASE CROSS ONE BOX IN EACH COLUMN	Children aged under 5	Children aged 5 to 15
No children	93.2	85.5
One child	4.5	7.4
Two children	1.8	5.3
Three children	0.4	1.4
More than three children	0.1	0.4

Q62. Which of these best describes the place where you live? PLEASE CROSS ONE BOX	
A big city	16.5
The suburbs or outskirts of a big city	14.6
A small city or town	37.9
A country village	23.3
A farm or home in the country	7.6

Q63. Please provide us with the first part of your postcode, e.g. if your post code is EH11 1AA, then write EH11 in the boxes below.

Q64. Finally, if you have any further comments to make about SNP membership, or about this questionnaire, please write them in the space below (continuing overleaf if required).

Thank you very much for taking the time to complete the questionnaire. Your help is greatly appreciated. Please return it in the pre-paid envelope provided to the address on the front of the questionnaire.

Data and Methods

The survey

The administration of the postal survey followed Dillman's (2000) 'tailored-design' method for maximizing response to postal questionnaires. This involves a personalized covering letter emphasizing the importance of the response, careful design of the questionnaire so as not to intimidate, confuse, or deter respondents, and a system of periodic follow-ups in the case of non-response. Closely parallel approaches were taken in the membership studies of the other parties in Britain.

A draft questionnaire for SNP members was produced in the Autumn of 2007. The questionnaire contained a number of questions asked of party members in earlier studies (Conservative, Labour, Liberal Democrat, and Green), as well as a number of questions from election studies and social surveys. However, the questionnaire contained many questions unique to the SNP and nationalism, to fully explore the nature of SNP membership. Following widespread consultation with academic colleagues and senior members of the SNP, the questionnaire was revised, then finalized, in October/November 2007. We would like to thank everyone involved in this process for their invaluable feedback.

The survey of SNP members involved a number of stages:

1. In November 2007 (08.11.07), the SNP's total membership stood at 13,203. Between 16 and 19 November 2007, a twenty-three-page questionnaire was sent to all members. The questionnaires were accompanied by a covering letter from the research team, and a letter from the party's Business Convener, Angus Robertson, as well as a pre-paid reply envelope. Royal Mail estimated that the questionnaires landed in mailboxes on Friday 23 November and the start of following week (w/c 26th). By the 5th of December, 2,888 completed questionnaires had been returned.

2. Reminder postcards were sent to those who had not yet responded between 5 and 7 December. By 21 December 2007, 5,327 questionnaires had been returned, a response rate of 40.3 per cent.

3. By 12 March 2008, the total responses had increased to 5,925 (44.9 per cent). At this stage, we conducted a third mailing. This involved mailing a fresh questionnaire and new covering letters, sent to all non-respondents (minus those who had contacted us to say they did not want to participate). This mailing took place Wednesday 12–Friday 14 March 2008.

4. In total, this final mailing led to an additional 1,187 questionnaires being returned. The final count in June 2008 was 7,112, a response rate of 53.9 per cent.

The response rate of the SNP survey compares favourably with those achieved in earlier surveys of party members in Britain (see table).

Party	Year	Sample	Returns	Response rate
Conservatives	1992	3,919	2,466	63.0
Greens (Brit)	1990	8,604	4,357	51.1
Greens (Scot)	1990	998 (all)	509	51.4
Greens (Scot)	2002	517 (all)	260	51.3
Labour	1989/90	8,075	5,065	62.5
Labour	1997	9,100	5,761	63.0
Liberal Democrats	1993	2,478	1,675	68.0
Liberal Democrats	1998/99	7,590	4,442	58.0
SNP	*2007/08*	*13,203*	*7,112*	*53.9*

Source: Rüdig et al. (1991, 1996); Seyd and Whiteley (1992, 2002); Whiteley et al. (1994); Whiteley et al. (2006); Bennie et al. (1996); Bennie (2004).

Bibliography

Achen, C. (1992), 'Social Psychology, Demographic Variables, and Linear Regression: Breaking the Iron Triangle in Voting Research', *Political Behaviour*, vol. 14, pp. 195–211.

Anderson, Benedict (1983), *Imagined Communities: Reflections on the Origin and Spread of Nationalism*, London: Verso.

Bechhofer, F. and D. McCrone (2010), 'Choosing National Identity', *Sociological Research Online*, vol. 15, pp. 1–15.

Beer, Samuel (1982), *Modern British Politics*, London: Faber and Faber.

Beiner, Ronald (ed.) (1999), *Theorizing Nationalism*, Albany: State University of New York.

Beller, Frank P. and Dennis C. Belloni (1978), 'Party and Faction: Modes of Political Competition', in F. Belloni and D. Beller (eds.), *Faction Politics: Political Parties and Factionalism in Comparative Perspective*, Oxford: ABC-CLIO Inc., pp. 417–50.

Bennie, L. (2004), *Understanding Political Participation: Green Party Membership in Scotland*, Aldershot: Ashgate.

—— J. Brand and J. Mitchell (1997), *How Scotland Votes*, Manchester: Manchester University Press.

—— J. Curtice and W. Rüdig (1996), 'Party Members', in D. McIver (ed.), *The Liberal Democrats*, Hemel Hempstead: Harvester Wheatsheaf, pp. 135–54.

—— D. Denver, J. Mitchell, and J. Bradbury (2001), 'Harbingers of New Politics? The Characteristics and Attitudes of Candidates in the Scottish Parliament Elections, 1999', *British Elections and Parties Review*, vol. 11, pp. 23–45.

Bochel, J.M. and D. Denver (1970), 'Religion and Voting: A Critical Review and a New Analysis', *Political Studies*, vol. 18, pp. 205–19.

Bowler, Shaun (2000), 'Parties in Legislatures: Two Competing Explanations', in R.J. Dalton and M. Wattenberg (eds.), *Parties without Partisans*, Oxford: Oxford University Press.

Bradbury, J, D. Denver, J. Mitchell, and L. Bennie (2000), 'Devolution and Party Change: Candidate Selection for the 1999 Scottish Parliament and Welsh Assembly Elections', *Journal of Legislative Studies*, vol. 6, pp. 51–72.

Brand, Jack (1978), *The National Movement in Scotland*, London: Routledge.

—— (1992), 'SNP Members: The Way of the Faithful', in P. Norris et al. (eds.), *British Elections and Parties Yearbook 1992*, Hemel Hempstead: Harvester Wheatsheaf, pp. 79–91.

——J. Mitchell (1993), 'Identity and the Vote: Class and Nationality in Scotland', *British Elections and Parties Yearbook, 1992*, Hemel Hempstead: Harvester Wheatsheaf, pp. 143–57.

Brown, A., D. McCrone, L. Paterson and P. Surridge (1999), *The Scottish Electorate: The 1997 General Election and Beyond*, London: MacMillan.

Brown, Oliver (1969), *Witdom*, Glasgow: Scotpress.

Brubaker, Roger (1992), *Citizenship and Nationhood in France and Germany*, Cambridge, MA: Harvard University Press.

Bruter, Michael and Sarah Harrison (2009a), *The Future of Our Democracies: Young Party Members in Europe*, Basingstoke: Palgrave MacMillan.

——— (2009b), 'Tomorrow's Leaders? Understanding the Involvement of Young Party Members in Six European Democracies', *Comparative Political Studies*, vol. 42, no. 10, pp. 1259–91.

Budge, Ian and Derek Urwin (1966), *Scottish Political Behaviour*, London: Longmans.

Bulmer, Elliot (2011), 'The Scottish National Party's Draft Constitution for Scotland: A Rejection of the Westminster Model?', *Parliamentary Affairs*, forthcoming.

Butler, David and Donald Stokes (1974), *Political Change in Britain*, London: Macmillan.

Calhoun, Craig (2007), *Nations Matter: Culture, History, and the Cosmopolitan Dream*, London: Routledge.

Calman, Sir Kenneth (Chair) (2009), *Serving Scotland Better: Scotland and the United Kingdom in the 21st Century*, Final Report, Edinburgh: Commission on Scottish Democracy.

Carty, Kenneth (2004), 'Parties as Franchise Systems: The Stratarchical Organizational Imperative', *Party Politics*, vol. 10, pp. 5–24.

Clark, A. (2006), *Local Parties, Participation and Campaigning in Post-Devolution Scotland*, PhD thesis, University of Aberdeen.

Clarke, P.B. and J.Q. Wilson (1961), 'Incentive Systems: A Theory of Organization', *Administrative Science Quarterly*, vol. 6, pp. 129–66.

Connor, W. (2001), 'From a Theory of Relative Economic Deprivation towards a Theory of Relative Political Deprivation', in M. Keating and J. McGarry (eds.), *Minority Nationalism and the Changing International Order*, Oxford: Oxford University Press.

Converse, P.E. and G. Dupeux (1962), 'Politicization of the Electorate in France and the United States', *Public Opinion Quarterly*, vol. 26, pp. 1–23.

Cornford, James and Jack Brand (1969), 'Scottish Voting Behaviour', in J.M. Wolfe (ed.), *Government and Nationalism in Scotland*, Edinburgh: Edinburgh University Press.

Cornock, Edward (2003), *The Political Mobilisation of the Working Class in Post-Devolution Scotland: A Case Study of the Scottish Socialist Party*, unpublished Open University PhD.

Crawford, Robert (1982), *The Scottish National Party, 1960–1974: An Investigation Into Its Organisation and Power Structure*, Unpublished Glasgow University PhD.

Creswell, J. (1994), *Research Design: Qualitative and Quantitative Approaches*, Thousand Oaks, CA: Sage.

Crewe, I. B. Sarlvik and J. Alt (1977), 'Partisan Dealignment in Britain, 1964–1974', *British Journal of Political Science*, vol. 7, pp. 129–90.

Cross, William and Lisa Young (2004), 'The Contours of Political Party Membership in Canada', *Party Politics*, vol. 10, pp. 427–44.

—— (2008), 'Activism Among Young Party Members: The Case of the Canadian Liberal Party', *Journal of Elections, Public Opinion and Parties*, vol. 18, no. 3, pp. 257–82.

Curtice, John (2006), 'Is Holyrood Accountable and Representative?', in Catherine Bromley, John Curtice, David McCrone, and Alison Park (eds.), *Has Devolution Delivered?* Edinburgh: Edinburgh University Press, pp. 90–108.

—— Michael Marsh, David McCrone, Nicola McEwen, and Rachel Ormston (2009), *Revolution or Evolution? The 2007 Scottish Elections*, Edinburgh: Edinburgh University Press.

—— D. Seawright (1995), 'The Decline of the Scottish Conservative and Unionist Party, 1950–1992', *Contemporary Record: The Journal of the Institute of Contemporary British History*, vol. 9, pp. 319–42.

Dalton, R.J. and M.P. Wattenberg (2000), *Parties Without Partisans: Political Change in Advanced Industrial Democracies*, Oxford: Oxford University Press.

Dalyell, Tam (1977), *Devolution, the End of Britain?* London: Jonathan Cape.

Denver, David, Gordon Hands and Iain MacAllister (2004), 'The Electoral Impact of Constituency Campaigning in Britain, 1992–2001, *Political Studies*, vol. 52, no. 2, pp. 289–306.

De Winter, L. (ed.) (1994), *Non-Statewide Parties in Europe*, Barcelona: ICPS.

De Winter, L. (1998), 'A Comparative Analysis of Electoral, Office and Policy Success of Ethnoregionalist Parties', in L. De Winter and H. Tursan (eds.), *Regionalist Parties in Western Europe*, London: Routledge.

—— M. Gómez-Reino and P. Lynch (2006), *Autonomist Parties in Europe: Identity Politics and the Revival of the Territorial Cleavage*, London: Routledge.

—— H. Tursan (eds.) (1998), *Regionalist Parties in Western Europe*, London: Routledge.

Downs, A. (1957), *An Economic Theory of Democracy*, New York: Harper.

Duverger, Maurice (1964), *Political Parties*, London: Methuen.

Elias, A. and F. Tronconi (2009), *Minority Nationalist Parties and the Challenges of Political Representation: A Framework of Analysis*, Cardiff: University of Wales Press.

Evans, Geoffrey, Anthony Heath, and Mansur Lalljee (1996), 'Measuring Left–Right and Libertarian–Authoritarian Values in the British Electorate', *British Journal of Sociology*, vol. 47, no. 1, pp. 93–112.

Fairlie, Jim (1990), 'Independence in Europe', Paper produced for meeting of SNP National Assembly, 9 December.

Finlay, Richard (1994), *Independent and Free: Scottish Politics and the Origins of the Scottish National Party, 1918–1945*, Edinburgh: John Donald.

Fisher, Justin and David Denver (2009), 'Evaluating the Electoral Effects of Traditional and Modern Modes of Constituency Campaigning in Britain', *Parliamentary Affairs*, vol. 62, pp. 196–210.

Gallagher, Michael (1988), 'Conclusion', in M. Gallagher and M. Marsh, *Candidate Selection in Comparative Perspective: The Secret Garden of Politics*, London: Sage.

—— M. Marsh (1988), *Candidate Selection in Comparative Perspective: The Secret Garden of Politics*, London: Sage.

—— —— (2002), *Days of Blue Loyalty: The Politics of Membership of the Fine Gael Party*, Dublin: PSAI Press.

Gallie, W.B. (1956), 'Essentially Contested Concepts'. *Proceedings of the Aristotelian Society*, vol. 56, pp. 167–98.

Gellner, Ernest (1983), *Nations and Nationalism*, Oxford: Basil Blackwell.

Gibson, Rachel and Stephen Ward (2000), *Reinvigorating Government? British Politics and the Internet*, Aldershot: Ashgate.

Goerres, Achim (2009), *The Political Participation of Older People in Europe: The Greying of Our Democracies*, Basingstoke: Palgrave Macmillan.

Goffman, Erving (1959), *The Presentation of Self in Everyday Life*, New York: Doubleday Anchor.

—— (1961), *Encounters*, Indianapolis: Bobbs-Merrill.

Gray, Charles (2002), 'From War of Attrition to Roller-coaster Ride: Local and central Government in Scotland', *Public Money and Management*, vol. 22, pp. 6–8.

Halliday, James (2000), *Scots Independent*, February 2000, no. 853.

—— (2011), *Memoirs*, Unpublished memoirs.

Hanham, H.J. (1969), *Scottish Nationalism*, London: Faber.

Harvie, Christopher (2004), *Scotland and Nationalism*, 4th edition, Abingdon: Routledge.

Hazan, R.Y. and G. Rahat (2006), 'Candidate Selection: Methods and Consequences', in Richard Katz and William Crotty (eds.), *Handbook of Party Politics*, London: Sage, pp. 109–21.

Hepburn, Eve (2009), 'Introduction: Re-conceptualizing Sub-state Mobilization', *Regional and Federal Studies*, vol. 19, pp. 477–99.

Ignatieff, Michael (1994), *Blood and Belonging: Journeys into the New Nationalism*, London: Vintage.

Johns, R., L. Bennie, and J. Mitchell (2011), 'Gendered Nationalism: The Gender Gap in Support for the Scottish National Party', *Party Politics*.

—— David Denver, James Mitchell and Charles Pattie (2010), *Voting for a Scottish Government*, Manchester: Manchester University Press.

—— James Mitchell and Lynn Bennie (2010), 'Gendered Nationalism: Gender Gap in Support for the Scottish National Party, *Party Politics*, forthcoming.

Johnson, P.E. (1998), 'Interest Group Recruiting: Finding Members and Recruiting Them', in A.J. Cigler and B. Loomis (eds.), *Interest Group Politics*, 5th edition, Washington, DC: Congressional Quarterly Inc., pp. 35–62.

Jordan, G. and W.A. Maloney (1997), *The Protest Business*, Manchester: Manchester University Press.

—— and W.A. Maloney (2007), *Democracy and Interest Groups: Enhancing Participation?* London: Palgrave MacMillan.

Katz, Richard (2001), 'The Problem of Candidate Selection and Models of Party Democracy', *Party Politics*, vol. 7, pp. 277–96.

—— —— and Peter Mair (1992), 'The Membership of Political Parties in European Democracies, 1960–1990', *European Journal of Political Research*, vol. 22, pp. 329–45.

Katz, R.S. and P. Mair (1995), 'Changing Models of Party Organization and Party Democracy', *Party Politics*, vol. 1, pp. 5–28.

Keating, Michael (1996), *Nations against the State. The New Politics of Nationalism in Quebec, Catalonia and Scotland*, Basingstoke: Macmillan.

—— (2009), *The Independence of Scotland*, Oxford: Oxford University Press.

Kellas, James (1971), 'Scottish Nationalism', in David Butler and Michael Pinto-Duschinsky, *The British General Election of 1970*, London: MacMillan, pp. 446–62.

Kendrick, S. (1983), *Social Change and Nationalism in Modern Scotland*, PhD dissertation, University of Edinburgh.

Kenny, M. and F. Mackay (2010), 'Increase in Women MPs in Scotland – Analysis of the Election', Engender, http://www.engender.org.uk/news/211/Increase_in_women_MPs_in_Scotland_-_anlaysis_of_the_election.html

Kiely, R., F. Bechhofer, R. Stewart, and D. McCrone (2001), 'The Markers and Rules of Scottish National Identity', *The Sociological Review*, vol. 49, pp. 33–55.

Kitschelt, H. (1986), 'Political Opportunity Structures and Political Protest: Anti-nuclear Movements in Four Democracies', *British Journal of Political Science*, vol. 16, pp. 57–85.

—— (1994), *The Transformation of European Social Democracy*, Cambridge: Cambridge University Press.

Kohn, Hans (1944), *The Idea of Nationalism*, New York: MacMillan.

Koole, Ruud (1996), 'Carde, Catch-all or Cartel? A Comment on the Notion of the Cartel Party', *Party Politics*, vol. 2, pp. 507–23.

Krouwel, André (2006), 'Party Models', in R.S. Katz and W. Crotty (eds.), *Handbook of Party Politics*, London: Sage.

Kuzio, Taras (2002), 'The Myth of the Civic State: A Critical Survey of Hans Kohn's Framework for Understanding Nationalism', *Ethnic and Racial Studies*, vol. 25, pp. 20–39.

Levy, Roger (1990), *Scottish Nationalism at the Crossroads*, Edinburgh: Scottish Academic Press.

Lucardie, Paul and Benoît Rihoux (2008), 'From Amateur-Activist to Professional-Electoral Parties? On the Organizational Transformation of Green Parties in Western Democracies', in E.G. Frankland, P. Lucardie, B. Rihoux (eds.), *Green Parties in Transition: The End of Grass-Roots Democracy?* Farnham: Ashgate.

Lynch, Peter (1996), *Minority Nationalism and European Integration*, Cardiff: University of Wales Press.

—— (2002), *SNP: The History of the Scottish National Party*, Cardiff: Welsh Academic Press.

Lynch, Peter (2009), 'From Social Democracy back to No Ideology? – The Scottish National Party and Ideological Change in a Multi-level Electoral Setting', *Regional and Federal Studies*, vol. 19, pp. 619–37.

MacAskill, Kenny (2004), *Building a Nation: Post Devolution Nationalism in Scotland*, Edinburgh: Luath Press.

MacCormick, John (1955), *Flag in the Wind*, London: Victor Gollancz.

MacCormick, Neil (1982), *Legal Right and Social Democrac: Essays in Legal and Political Philosophy*, Oxford: Clarendon Press.

—— (1999), *Questioning Sovereignty*, Oxford: Oxford University Press.

—— (2000), 'Is there a Constitutional Pat to Scottish Independence?', *Parliamentary Affairs*, vol. 53, pp. 721–36.

MacLeod, D. and M. Russell (2006), *Grasping the Thistle*, Glendaruel: Argyll Publishing.

Mair, P. (1994), 'Party Organizations: From Civil Society to State', in R.S. Katz and P. Mair (eds.), *How Parties Organise: Change and Adaptation in Part Organizations in Western Democracies*, London: Sage, pp. 1–22.

—— C. Muddie (1998), 'The Party Family and its Study', *Annual Review of Political Science*, vol. 1, pp. 211–29.

—— I. Van Beizen (2001), 'Party Membership in Twenty European Democracies', 1980–2000', *Party Politics*, vol. 7, pp. 5–21.

Maloney, W. (2009), 'Interest Groups and the Revitalisation of Democracy: Are We Expecting Too Much?', *Representation*, vol. 45, pp. 277–88.

Mansbach, R. W. (1972), 'The SNP: A Revised Political Profile', *Comparative Politics*, vol. 5, pp. 185–210.

—— (1973), 'The Scottish National Party', *Comparative Politics*, vol. 5, pp. 185–210.

March, James G. and Olsen, Johan P. (1989), *Rediscovering Institutions: The Organizational Basis of Politics*, New York: Free Press.

Margetts, Helen (2010), 'The Internet in Political Science', in Colin Hay (ed.), *New Directions in Political Science: Responding to the Challenges of an Interdependent World*, Houndmills, Basingstoke: Palgrave MacMillan, pp. 64–87.

Markus, G.B. and Converse, P.E. (1979), A Dynamic Simultaneous Equation Model of Electoral Choice', *American Political Science Review*, vol. 73, pp. 1055–70.

Marsh, Michael (2004), 'None of Your Post-modern Stuff around Here: Grassroots Campaigning in the 2002 Irish General Elections', in David Broughton, Justin Fisher, Roger Scully, Paul Webb (eds.), *British Elections and Parties Review Volume 14*, London: Frank Cass, pp. 245–67.

Massetti, Emanuele (2009), 'Explaining Regional Party Positioning in a Multi-dimensional Ideological Space: A Framework for Analysis', *Regional and Federal Studies*, vol. 19, pp. 501–31.

Maxwell, Stephen (1985), 'The 79 Group: A Critical Retrospect', *Cencrastus*, vol. 21, pp. 11–16.

May, John D. (1973), 'Opinion Structure of Political Parties: The Special Law of Curvilear Disparity', *Political Studies*, vol. 21, pp. 135–51.

McAdam, Doug (1996), 'Conceptual Origins, Current Problems, Future Directions', in D. McAdam, J.D. McCarthy, and M.N. Zald, *Comparative Perspectives on Social Movements: Political Opportunities, Mobilizing Structures, and Cultural Framings*, Cambridge: Cambridge University Press, pp. 23–40.

McAllister, Ian (1981), 'Party Organization and Minority Nationalism: A Comparative Study in the United Kingdom', *European Journal of Political Research*, vol. 9, pp. 237–55.

McCrone, David (1988), *The Sociology of Nationalism*, London: Routledge.

—— (2001), *Understanding Scotland: The Sociology of a Nation*, 2nd edition, London: Routledge.

—— F. Bechhofer (2008), 'National Identity and Social Inclusion', *Ethnic and Racial Studies*, vol. 31, pp. 1245–66.

McEwen, N. (2002), 'The Scottish National Party after Devolution: Progress and Prospects', in G. Hassan and C. Warhurst (eds.), *Tomorrow's Scotland*, London: Lawrence and Wishart.

McLean, Iain (1970), 'The Rise and Fall of the SNP', *Political Studies*, vol. 18, pp. 367–72.

Meinecke, Friedrich ([1907] 1970), *Cosmopolitanism and the National State*, Princeton, NJ: Princeton University Press.

Melucci, A. (1984), 'An End to Social Movements? An Introductory Paper to the Sessions on "New Social Movements and Change in Organizational Forms"', *Social Science Information*, vol. 23, pp. 819–35.

Merrill, Samuel, Bernard Grofman, and James Adams (2001), 'Assimilation and Contrast Effects in Voter Projections of Party Locations: Evidence from Norway, France and the USA', *European Journal of Political Research*, vol. 40, pp. 199–221.

Miller, Dale T., Brian Taylor, and Michelle L. Buck (1991), 'Gender Gaps: Who Needs to be Explained?', *Journal of Personality and Social Psychology*, vol. 61, pp. 5–12.

Miller, William (1981), *The End of British Politics?* Oxford: Clarendon Press.

Mishler, William and Anthony Mughan (1978), 'Representing the Celtic Fringe: Devolution and Legislative Behavior in Scotland and Wales', *Legislative Studies Quarterly*, vol. 3, pp. 377–408.

Mitchell, James (1988), 'Recent Developments in the Scottish National Party', in *Political Quarterly*, vol. 59, pp. 473–7.

—— (1990), 'Factions, Tendencies and Consensus in the SNP in the 1980s', *Scottish Government Yearbook 1990*, Edinburgh: Edinburgh University Press, pp. 49–61.

—— (1996), *Strategies for Self-Government*, Edinburgh: Polygon.

—— (1998), 'Member State or Euro-Region? The SNP, Plaid Cymru, and Europe', in David Baker and David Seawright (eds.), *Britain For And Against Europe: British Politics and the Question of European Integration*, Oxford: Clarendon Press, pp. 108–29.

—— (2009a), *Devolution in the United Kingdom*, Manchester: Manchester University Press.

Mitchell, James (2009b), 'From Breakthrough to Mainstream: The Politics of Potential and Blackmail', in G. Hassan (eds.), *The Modern SNP: From Protest To Power*, Edinburgh: Edinburgh University Press, pp. 31–41.

—— L. Bennie (1996), 'Thatcherism and the Scottish Question', *British Elections and Parties Yearbook, 1995*, Ilford, Essex: Frank Cass, pp. 90–104.

—— R. Johns, and L. Bennie (2009), 'Who are the SNP Members?', in G. Hassan (ed.), *The Modern SNP: From Protest to Power*, Edinburgh: Edinburgh University Press, pp. 68–78.

Morales, Laura (2009), *Joining Political Organisations: Institutions, Mobilisation and Participation in Western Democracies*, Colchester: ECPR Press.

Murkens, Jo, Peter Jones, and Michael Keating (2002), *Scottish Independence, Legal and Constitutional Issues: A Practical Guide*, Edinburgh: Edinburgh University Press.

Murray, G. and Tonge, J. (2005), *Sinn Fein and the SDLP: From Alienation to Participation*, London: Hurst.

Nieguth, Tim (1999), 'Beyond Dichotomy: Concepts of the Nation and the Distribution of Membership', *Nations and Nationalism*, vol. 5, pp. 155–73.

Norman, Wayne (2006), *Negotiating Nationalism*, Oxford: Oxford University Press.

Norris, Pippa (1995), 'May's Law of Curvilinear Disparity Revisited', *Party Politics*, vol. 1, pp. 29–47.

Oates, Sarah, Diana Owen, and Rachel Gibson (eds.) (2006), *The Internet and Politics: Citizens, Voters and Activists*, Abingdon: Routledge.

Office of Chief Statistician (2004), *Analysis of Ethnicity in The 2001 Census: Summary Report*, Edinburgh: Scottish Executive.

Olson, M. (1965), *The Logic of Collective Action*, Cambridge MA: Harvard University Press.

—— (1971), *The Logic of Collective Action*, revised edition, New York: Schocken Books.

Özkirimli, Umut (2005), *Contemporary Debates on Nationalism: A Critical Engagement*, Basingstoke: Palgrave Macmillan.

Panebianco, Angelo (1988), *Political Parties: Organization and Power*, Cambridge: Cambridge University Press.

Party Politics (2004), *Party Members and Activists*, special edition, vol. 10, no. 4.

Paterson, L. (2006), 'Sources of Support for the SNP', in C. Bromley, J. Curtice, D. McCrone, and A. Park (eds.), *Has Devolution Delivered?*, Edinburgh: Edinburgh University Press, pp. 46–68.

—— A. Brown, J. Curtis, K. Hinds, D. McCrone, A. Park, K. Sprotson, and P. Surridge (2001), *New Scotland, New Politics*, Edinburgh: Polygon.

Patton, M. (1990), *Qualitative Evaluation and Research Methods*, 2nd edition, Newbury Park, CA: Sage.

Peters, B. Guy (1999), *Institutional Theory in Political Science: The 'New Institutionalism*, London: Pinter.

Pfaff, William (1993), *The Wrath of Nations*, London: Simon & Schuster.

Plamenatz, John (1973), 'Two Types of Nationalism', in E. Kamenka (ed.), *Nationalism. The Nature and Evolution of an Idea*, London: Edward Arnold.

Poguntke, Thomas (1993), *Alternative Politics: The German Green Party*, Edinburgh: Edinburgh University Press.

Pulzer, Peter (1968), *Political Representation and Elections in Britain*, London: George Allen & Unwin.

Rahat, G. and R.Y. Hazan (2001), 'Candidate Selection Methods: An Analytical Framework', *Party Politics*, vol. 7, pp. 297–322.

Read, M. and D. Marsh (2002), 'Combining Qualitative and Quantitative Methods', in D. Marsh and G. Stoker, *Theory and Methods in Political Science*, 2nd edition, Houndmills: Palgrave MacMillan, pp. 231–48.

Rose, Richard (1964), 'Parties, Factions and Tendencies in Britain', *Political Studies*, vol. 12, p. 38, pp. 33–46.

——Tom Mackie (1988), 'Do Parties Persist or Fail? The Big Trade-off Facing Organizations', in Merkl, P. and Lawson, K. (eds.), *When Parties Fail: Emerging Alternative Organizations*, Princeton, NJ: Princeton University Press, pp. 533–58.

Rüdig, W., L. Bennie, and M. Franklin (1991), *Green Party Members: A Profile*, Glasgow: Delta Publications.

——M. Franklin, and L. Bennie (1996), 'Up and Down with the Greens: Ecology and Politics in Britain 1989–1992', *Electoral Studies*, vol. 15, no. 1, pp. 1–20.

Russell, M. (2005), *The Politics of Party Organisation: Building New Labour*, Basingstoke: Palgrave Macmillan.

Russell, Michael (2004), 'Swinney could Face "Men in Grey Kilts" ', *Sunday Herald*, 4 April.

Salmond, Alex (2007), 'Speech by Alex Salmond, Council on Foreign Relations', New York, http://www.cfr.org/publication/14497/speech_by_alex_salmond_first_minister_of_scotland.html, 12 October.

Sartori, G. (1976), *Parties and Party Systems: A Framework for Analysis*, Cambridge: Cambridge University Press.

Scarrow, Susan (1996), *Parties and their Members: Organizing for Victory in Britain and Germany*, Oxford: Oxford University Press.

——(2000), 'Parties without Members? Party Organization in a Changing Electoral Environment', in Dalton, Russell and Martin Wattenberg (eds.), *Parties Without Partisans*, Oxford: Oxford University Press, pp. 79–101.

——Burcu Gezgor (2010), 'Declining Memberships, Changing Members? European Political Party Members in a New Era', *Party Politics*, vol. 16, no. 6, pp. 823–43.

——Paul Webb and David Farrell (2000), 'From Social Integration to Electoral Contestation: The Changing Distribution of Power within Political Parties', in Russell J. Dalton and Martin P. Wattenberg (eds.), *Parties without Partisans: Political Change in Advanced Industrial Democracies*, Oxford: Oxford University Press, pp. 129–51.

Schattschneider, E.E. (1960 [1942]), *Party Government*, New York: Holt, Rinehart, and Winston.

Schulman, Stephen (2002), 'Challenging the Civic/Ethnic and West/East Dichotomies in the Study of Nationalism', *Comparative Political Studies*, vol. 35, pp. 554–85.

Schuman, H., L. Bobo, and M. Krysan (1992), 'Authoritarianism in the General Population: The Education Interaction Hypothesis', *Social Psychology Quarterly*, vol. 55, pp. 379–87.

Schwarz, John (1970), 'The Scottish National Party: Nonviolent Separatism and Theories of Violence', *World Politics*, vol. 22, pp. 496–517.

Sears, David O., Richard R. Lau, Tom R. Tyler, and Harris M. Allen, Jr. (1980), 'Self-interest vs. Symbolic Politics in Policy Attitudes and Presidential Voting', *American Political Science Review*, vol. 74, pp. 670–84.

Seyd, P. and P. Whiteley (1992), *Labour's Grass Roots: The Politics of Party Membership*, Oxford: Clarendon.

—— —— (1995), 'Labour and Conservative Party Members: Change Over Time, *Parliamentary Affairs*, vol. 48, no. 3, pp. 456–71.

—— —— (2002), *New Labour's Grassroots: The Transformation of the Labour Party Membership*, Basingstoke: Palgrave MacMillan.

—— —— (2004), 'British Party Members: An Overview', *Party Politics*, vol. 10, no. 4, pp. 427–44.

Sillars, Jim (1989), *Independence in Europe*, Glasgow: Jim Sillars.

—— (1990), 'Scottish Independence in Europe', Edinburgh: Scottish National Party.

Smith, Anthony (1991), *National Identity*, London: Penguin.

SNP (1974), *General Election Manifesto*, Edinburgh: Scottish National Party.

—— (1976), *SNP Conference Proceedings 1976*, Edinburgh: Scottish National Party.

—— (1979), *SNP Conference Proceedings 1979*, Edinburgh: Scottish National Party.

—— (1981), *SNP Conference Proceedings 1981*, Edinburgh: Scottish National Party.

—— (1983), *SNP Conference Proceedings 1983*, Edinburgh: Scottish National Party.

—— (1997), *National Council Resolutions*, 2 August, Edinburgh: Scottish National Party.

—— (2002), *A Constitution for a Free Scotland*, Edinburgh: Scottish National Party.

—— (2004a), *SNP Constitution*, Edinburgh: Scotish National Party.

—— (2004b), *Mid-Year Reports 2005 and Financial Statement 2004*, Edinburgh: Scottish National Party.

—— (2004c), Leadership Election Rules, Edinburgh: Scottish National Party.

—— (2009), *Annual Review 2008/09*, Edinburgh: Scottish National Party.

Somerville, Paula (2009), *A History of the Scottish National Party, 1945–67*, Unpublished Strathclyde University PhD.

Swinney, John (2003), 'Speech to SNP Conference', September 26.

Tashakkori, A. and C. Teddlie (1998), *Mixed Methodology: Combining Qualitative and Quantitative Approaches*, Thousand Oaks, CA: Sage.

Tilley, James (2005), 'Liberatarian–Authoritarian Value Change in Britain, 1974–2001', *Political Studies*, vol. 53, pp. 442–53.

Tonge, J. (2005), *The New Northern Irish Politics?* Houndmills: Palgrave MacMillan.

—— (2006), *Northern Ireland*, Cambridge: Polity.

Tonge, J. Evans (2001), 'Faultlines in Unionism: Division and Dissent within the Ulster Unionist Council', *Irish Political Studies*, vol. 16, pp. 111–32.

——— (2002), 'Party Members and the Good Friday Agreement in Northern Ireland', *Irish Political Studies*, vol. 17, pp. 59–73.

Triandafyllidou, A. (1988), 'National Identity and the "Other" ', *Ethnic and Racial Studies*, vol. 21, pp. 593–612.

Urwin, Derek (1994), 'Back to the Future – Again? A Reassessment of Minority Nationalism in Western Democracies', *Journal of Behavioral and Social Sciences*, vol. 1994, pp. 1–23.

van der Zwet, Arno (2010), 'Sheep in Wolves' Clothing? Definitions of the Nation in the Scottish National Party and Frisian National Party', Paper presented at the ECPR Graduate Conference 2010.

Verba, S, K.L. Schlozman, and H.E. Brady (1995), *Voice and Equality: Civic Voluntarism in American Politics*, Harvard: Harvard University Press.

Webb, Keith and Eric Hall (1978), 'Explanations of the Rise of Political Nationalism in Scotland', University of Strathclyde, *Studies in Public Policy*, no. 15.

Webb, Paul (2000), *The Modern British Party System*, London: Sage.

——— D. Farrell, and I. Holliday (2002), *Political Parties in Advanced Industrial Democracies*, Oxford: Oxford University Press.

Whiteley, Paul (2009), 'Where Have All the Members Gone? The Dynamics of Party Membership in Britain', *Parliamentary Affairs*, vol. 66, no. 2, pp. 242–57.

——— P. Seyd (1998), 'The Dynamics of Party Activism in Britain – A Spiral of Demobilisation?', *British Journal of Political Science*, vol. 28, pp. 113–37.

——— (2002), *High-Intensity Participation: the Dynamic of Party Activism in Britain*, Ann Arbor, MI: University of Michigan Press.

——— M. Billinghurst (2006), *Third Force Politics: Liberal Democrats at the Grassroots*, Oxford: Oxford University Press.

——— J. Richardson (1994), *True Blues: The Politics of Conservative Party Membership*, Oxford: Clarendon.

Widfeldt, Anders (1995), 'Party Membership and Party Representativeness', in H.D. Klingemann and D. Fuchs (eds.), *Citizens and the State*, Oxford: Oxford University Press.

——— (1999), *Linking Parties with People? Party Membership in Sweden 1960–1997*, Aldershot: Ashgate.

Wilson, Gordon (2009), *SNP: The Turbulent Years, 1960–1990*, Stirling: Scots Independent.

Wilson, J.Q. (1995), *Political Organizations*, Princeton, NJ: Princeton University Press.

Wolfe, Billy (1973), *Scotland Lives*, Edinburgh: Reprographia.

——— (1976), *Chairman's Report*, SNP National Council, 4 September.

——— (1979), 'Comment on SNP Results and on Matters Affecting them', SNP Internal Memorandum.

Yack, Bernard (1999), 'The Myth of the Civic Nation', in R. Beiner (ed.), *Theorizing Nationalism*, Albany: State University of New York.

Index

Index